THE LAS V

POCKET GUIDE 2025

Insider Tips, Must-See Attractions, and Hidden Gems for Your Ultimate Vegas Experience

Globetrail Guides

English Edition

TABLE OF CONTENTS

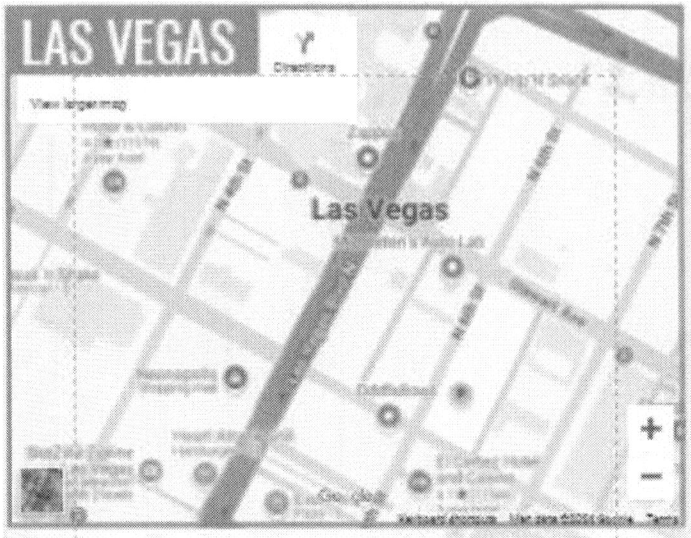

SCAN THE QR CODE

- Open your phone's camera.
- Point it at the QR code.
- Wait for the notification.
- Tap the link or prompt.
- Follow the instructions.

INTRODUCTION

My first trip to Las Vegas in 2024 was more than I imagined an unforgettable experience from start to finish. The moment I stepped onto the famous Strip, I was mesmerized by the towering hotels, bright neon lights, and lively crowds. It felt like stepping into a different world, one full of energy, excitement, and endless possibilities. The atmosphere was infectious, and I knew right away I was in for an adventure.

My first night was spent wandering the Strip, taking in the sights and sounds. The Bellagio's fountain left me speechless, with its water dancing in sync with music against the backdrop of the illuminated city. I then headed to a rooftop bar, sipping a cocktail while enjoying a view of the dazzling city below. Everything seemed so alive, and I couldn't help but smile at the beauty around me.

The next day, I went beyond the Strip and found myself in Downtown Las Vegas. The Fremont Street Experience was something I'll never forget. It was colorful and fun, with street performers, live music, and an exciting atmosphere. I even took the SlotZilla zipline, soaring above the crowd as people cheered from below. It felt exhilarating and gave me a unique view of the historic heart of Vegas.

A surprising highlight was my trip to Red Rock Canyon. Just a short drive from the city, the stunning desert landscape offered a peaceful escape from the buzzing city life. As I hiked the trails, surrounded by towering red rocks, I felt completely at peace a perfect contrast to the nonstop energy of Las Vegas.

As my trip came to an end, I treated myself to an amazing dinner at a Michelin-starred restaurant. The food was incredible, and it was the perfect way to wrap up my time in this unforgettable city.

Las Vegas has so much more to offer than I could have imagined adventure, beauty, excitement, and even tranquility. If you're planning a trip, this book has everything you need to make your experience just as amazing. Whether it's your first visit or your fifth, the magic of Vegas will never fail to surprise and delight.

CHAPTER 1: DISCOVERING LAS VEGAS

A Brief History of the Entertainment Capital of the World

Las Vegas, often called the "Entertainment Capital of the World," has a fascinating history that has shaped it into the vibrant city it is today. Founded in 1905, Las Vegas began as a small railroad town in the Mojave Desert, providing a critical stop between Los Angeles and Salt Lake City. Its early significance was tied to this strategic location and the abundant artesian wells that made life possible in such a dry, arid climate.

The real turning point for Las Vegas came in 1931 when the state of Nevada legalized gambling. This pivotal decision transformed the city's future. Around the same time, the construction of the Hoover Dam brought thousands of workers to the area, fueling the local economy and providing jobs. These workers and the newly legalized gambling helped lay the foundation for Las Vegas' thriving casino culture.

The 1940s and 1950s marked a glamorous era for Las Vegas. Organized crime families began investing heavily in building hotels and casinos, contributing to the construction of famous landmarks like the Flamingo Hotel, which was one of the first luxurious resorts on the Strip. These casinos weren't just gambling dens; they were palatial resorts that attracted stars and tourists alike. Mob figures such as Bugsy Siegel played a significant role in shaping this era of Las Vegas, blending crime with glitz and glamour. Celebrities from Frank Sinatra to Elvis Presley began to perform in these hotels, cementing Las Vegas as a hub for world-class entertainment.

Las Vegas' modern growth continued through the 1980s and 1990s, when a wave of corporate ownership took over the city's casinos, bringing family-friendly resorts into the mix. The massive themed hotels such as the Mirage, Treasure Island, and Excalibur catered to families while maintaining the adult allure that Sin City was famous for. The rise of mega-resorts, complete with elaborate shows, concerts, and Michelin-starred dining, defined this era and laid the groundwork for the Las Vegas we know today.

In the 21st century, Las Vegas evolved yet again, positioning itself as more than just a gambling destination. The city has become known for its high-end dining, shopping, luxury hotels, and entertainment that extends well beyond the casinos. Annual events like CES (Consumer Electronics Show) and Electric Daisy Carnival (EDC) have added a modern twist to the city's already extensive offerings.

Today, Las Vegas remains a symbol of excess, entertainment, and reinvention. Its history continues to influence its modern identity as it remains the largest city in Nevada and the seat of Clark County. The Strip is constantly changing, with old casinos being torn down and new ones rising in their place, yet the spirit of Las Vegas a city that thrives on dreams, risk, and reinvention endures.

Why Visit Las Vegas: A Year-Round Destination

Las Vegas is a city that never goes out of style, no matter the season. With its endless array of attractions, shows, and experiences, this vibrant destination offers something for everyone, all year long. Whether you're drawn to the summer heat or the cooler, festive winter months, Las Vegas has a charm that adapts to every season, making it a truly fantastic place to visit any time of the year.

For sun-seekers, summer in Las Vegas means epic pool parties, rooftop lounges, and sun-soaked adventures. The famous pool scenes at hotels like the MGM Grand, Caesars Palace, and Encore Beach Club come alive with DJs, refreshing cocktails, and an atmosphere that blends relaxation with celebration. Beyond the poolside fun, summer is also the perfect time for adventurous day trips to nearby natural wonders like Red Rock Canyon or Lake Mead, where you can cool off with water sports or hike through stunning landscapes.

As the temperatures drop, Las Vegas transforms into a winter wonderland filled with holiday cheer. Festive lights twinkle along the Strip, and special seasonal shows and events make this time of year truly magical. Wander through the enchanting displays at the Bellagio Conservatory, experience ice skating under the stars at The Cosmopolitan, or marvel at the giant holiday tree in the LINQ Promenade. New Year's Eve in Las Vegas is legendary, with jaw-dropping fireworks and celebrations that rival any in the world.

For those seeking to avoid the hustle and bustle, off-peak seasons like spring and fall offer the ideal opportunity to experience Las Vegas with fewer crowds and potentially lower prices on hotels and entertainment. Springtime brings perfect weather for exploring outdoor attractions, from the Valley of

Fire to the Hoover Dam, while the fall season is rich with cultural festivals, such as the Las Vegas Food & Wine Festival and Life is Beautiful, a multi-day celebration of music, art, and culinary delights.

Las Vegas is also a great destination for all ages, offering a variety of attractions to suit every interest. Families can enjoy kid-friendly adventures like the Shark Reef Aquarium at Mandalay Bay, the High Roller observation wheel, or the whimsical Adventuredome theme park at Circus Circus. Meanwhile, adults can indulge in everything from high-stakes casino action to luxurious spa treatments and endless shopping along the Strip.

No matter when you visit, Las Vegas guarantees an unforgettable experience. Its unique ability to cater to every traveler, from adrenaline junkies to relaxation enthusiasts, makes it the ultimate year-round destination. So whether you're looking for summer fun, festive winter celebrations, or a peaceful escape in the off-season, one thing is certain: any time is the perfect time to visit Las Vegas!

How to Use This Guide

This guide is your key to unlocking the full potential of your Las Vegas adventure in 2025. Whether you're a first-time visitor or a seasoned traveler, this book is designed to help you navigate the city, find hidden gems, and make the most of your time in this dynamic destination.

The guide is organized into clear sections to make it easy for you to find what you're looking for:

- **Top Attractions**: This section highlights the must-see sights on the Strip, from the iconic Bellagio Fountains to the Neon Museum. Whether you're drawn to Vegas' glitzy casinos or its historical landmarks, this part of the guide will ensure you don't miss any of the city's highlights.
- **Entertainment and Shows**: Las Vegas is world-renowned for its shows. Here, you'll find information on everything from Cirque du Soleil performances to the latest residencies of music superstars. This section includes helpful tips on how to get the best tickets at the best prices.
- **Dining**: Las Vegas offers some of the finest dining experiences in the world. From Michelin-starred

restaurants to budget-friendly buffets, the dining section provides reviews and recommendations to suit every taste and budget.

- **Where to Stay**: This section breaks down accommodation options, from luxurious suites at iconic hotels to budget-friendly stays. Whether you're looking for five-star resorts or practical places to stay, this section ensures you can find a place that fits your needs.
- **Casinos and Gambling**: If you're interested in trying your luck, the guide walks you through the various casinos, the types of games offered, and strategies for making the most of your gaming experience.
- **Shopping and Nightlife**: Find recommendations for high-end shopping, unique boutiques, and the best nightclubs to experience Vegas' vibrant after-dark scene.
- **Outdoor Activities and Day Trips**: Las Vegas isn't just about the Strip. This guide highlights outdoor excursions, such as hiking in Red Rock Canyon or visiting the Hoover Dam. There are also recommendations for day trips to nearby attractions like the Grand Canyon.
- **Family-Friendly Activities**: If you're traveling with kids, this section provides a list of family-friendly activities,

from amusement parks to aquariums, so everyone can enjoy the trip.

- **Local Culture and History**: For those looking to dive deeper into the city's history, this section explores Downtown Las Vegas, the Mob Museum, and cultural venues that offer a different view of the city.

To make the most of your stay, plan. Start by reading the **Itinerary Planning** chapter to create a day-by-day schedule tailored to your interests. Use the map and transportation tips to help you navigate the city efficiently. Don' t forget to check out the **Insider Tips** section, where you'll find information on seasonal events, hidden gems, and how to save money during your trip.

This guide is designed to be both informative and practical, giving you all the tools you need to have an unforgettable experience in Las Vegas. Whether you're here for a weekend getaway or an extended stay, this book will help you make the most of every moment.

Responsible Travel Tips & Safety Precautions

While Las Vegas is a city known for fun and adventure, it's important to keep safety and responsibility in mind to ensure a truly enjoyable experience. Whether you're navigating the lively nightlife or exploring the city's many attractions, following these responsible travel tips and safety precautions will help you make the most of your trip while staying safe and mindful of your impact on the environment and the local community.

Staying Safe While Enjoying the Nightlife

Las Vegas nightlife is legendary, and whether you're hitting the dance floor at a top nightclub or enjoying a cocktail at a chic rooftop bar, it's important to stay safe:

- **Stay with your group:** Stick with your friends or travel companions when going out, and agree on meeting points if you get separated.
- **Keep your belongings secure:** Be mindful of your belongings in crowded places. Use bags that close securely, and avoid carrying large amounts of cash.
- **Stay hydrated:** The desert heat, combined with alcohol consumption, can dehydrate you quickly. Drink water

regularly, especially during pool parties and outdoor events.

- **Know your limits:** It's easy to get caught up in the excitement, but drink responsibly and be aware of your alcohol tolerance.
- **Use safe transportation:** Rideshare services like Uber and Lyft are widely available. Avoid walking alone at night in unfamiliar areas, and always opt for a licensed taxi or rideshare.

Responsible Gambling Guidelines

Las Vegas casinos offer thrilling entertainment, but it's important to gamble responsibly:

- **Set a budget:** Before you hit the casino floor, decide on a budget and stick to it. Never gamble more than you can afford to lose.
- **Take breaks:** Gambling for extended periods can lead to poor decision-making. Step away from the tables to enjoy other attractions or grab a bite to eat.
- **Know the signs:** If you feel like gambling is becoming more than just entertainment, many casinos provide

resources for gambling addiction support, including hotlines and counseling.

- **Enjoy the games responsibly:** Gambling should be seen as a form of entertainment, not a way to make money. Have fun, but keep it in perspective!

Environmental Conservation Tips

While Las Vegas is a city of indulgence, there are simple ways to help minimize your environmental impact:

- **Reuse and recycle:** Many hotels offer recycling programs and encourage reusing towels and linens to conserve water and energy. Participate in these initiatives where possible.
- **Carry a reusable water bottle:** Staying hydrated is key in the desert, but you can reduce plastic waste by bringing a reusable bottle. Many hotels and public spaces have water refill stations.
- **Respect natural spaces:** If you plan to explore nearby outdoor attractions like Red Rock Canyon or Lake Mead, stick to designated trails and leave no trace. Dispose of trash properly and avoid disturbing wildlife.

- **Opt for energy-efficient transportation:** Consider using public transportation or carpooling to reduce your carbon footprint while moving around the city.

Supporting Local Business

While the Las Vegas Strip is packed with big-name hotels and casinos, the city also boasts a thriving local business scene:

- **Explore off-Strip attractions:** Visit local restaurants, boutiques, and art galleries in the downtown area or the Arts District to support small businesses.
- **Attend local events:** From farmers' markets to art shows and cultural festivals, attending community events is a great way to experience the local culture while supporting the city's small businesses.
- **Try local cuisine:** While celebrity chefs abound, you'll also find incredible food from locally owned restaurants serving everything from classic American fare to authentic international cuisine.

Practical Safety Information

Lastly, it's important to be prepared for any situation:

- **Emergency Contacts:** The local emergency number in Las Vegas is 911 for police, fire, or medical assistance.

- **Health Services:** There are several urgent care centers and hospitals located near the Strip, including Sunrise Hospital and University Medical Center, should you need medical attention.
- **Hotel Safety:** Familiarize yourself with the emergency exits in your hotel, and make sure to lock your door when leaving your room or retiring for the night.
- **Know the laws:** Be aware of local regulations, such as the legal drinking age of 21 and public smoking restrictions. Nevada also has strict laws about open containers of alcohol, so always check before walking around with a drink in hand.

By following these tips and precautions, you can ensure a safe, responsible, and enjoyable trip to Las Vegas. Whether you're here for the excitement of the Strip or to experience the city's hidden gems, traveling with care and mindfulness will enrich your adventure while helping preserve the beauty and vibrancy of this iconic destination.

CHAPTER 2: ICONIC ATTRACTIONS & LANDMARKS

The Las Vegas Strip: A Stroll Through Neon Paradise

Walking down the Las Vegas Strip is like stepping into a dream world bathed in neon. A glittering, larger-than-life boulevard that stretches for miles, the Strip is

the beating heart of Las Vegas an electric playground where every corner bursts with excitement, and every building shines brighter than the next. As you stroll along this iconic road, you'll find yourself surrounded by an endless kaleidoscope of flashing lights, dazzling marquees, and the constant hum of slot machines echoing from open casino doors. The air is alive with energy, a vibrant mix of music, laughter, and the collective buzz of anticipation.

The Strip's visual feast is unlike anything you've seen before. Towering skyscrapers, intricate replicas of global landmarks, and opulent resorts line both sides of the road, each competing for your attention. You'll pass by the mesmerizing fountains of the **Bellagio**, where water dances in perfect harmony to music and lights, creating a show that captivates all who gather around. Across the street, the Eiffel Tower at the **Paris Las Vegas** transports you to the City of Lights, a half-scale replica of the famous French landmark standing tall amidst the desert skyline.

The architecture of the Strip is a spectacle in itself. Each resort is designed as a world unto its own. At the **Venetian**, gondoliers glide through canals, serenading guests as they drift beneath bridges and past charming Italian facades. Just down the road, the pyramid-shaped **Luxor** rises majestically, its towering light beam shooting straight into the night sky, visible from miles away. Wander through the ancient streets of the **Caesars Palace** complex, where towering statues and Roman columns transport you back in time, yet somehow, you're still firmly rooted in the thrill of modern Las Vegas.

As you walk, the sounds of the Strip swirl around you. The cheerful ding of slot machines spills from the doors of iconic casinos like the **MGM Grand**, **The Mirage**, and **Wynn Las Vegas**, while street performers entertain passersby with magic tricks, music, and impromptu acts. You'll see a mix of visitors, from wide-eyed tourists taking in the grandeur for the first time to seasoned travelers navigating their favorite spots with ease. The Strip is a crossroads of cultures, languages, and styles, adding to the ever-present sense that you're in a place where anything is possible.

Beyond the casinos, the Strip offers countless must-visit establishments. Fine dining restaurants helmed by celebrity chefs, luxury shopping at **The Forum Shops at Caesars** or the **Shops at Crystals**, and world-renowned shows featuring everything from acrobatics to magic are all just steps away. Whether you're grabbing a quick bite from a famous food truck or indulging in a multi-course meal, Las Vegas promises culinary adventures to match its visual splendor.

The Strip is more than just a road it's a journey through fantasy, a neon-lit adventure where every step leads to something new and exciting. From its awe-inspiring architecture to its endless entertainment, a walk through the Las Vegas Strip is an experience that engages all your senses, leaving you dazzled, exhilarated, and ready for more. Here, in this neon paradise, the heart of Las Vegas beats strongest, calling visitors to revel in the magic of the moment.

Fremont Street Experience

Step back in time to the heart of *Old Vegas* with the Fremont Street Experience, where the glitz and glamour of the past still shine as brightly as the neon signs that line this historic downtown corridor. Long before the towering resorts and sleek casinos of the Strip, Fremont Street was the epicenter of Las Vegas excitement a place where legends were born, fortunes were made, and the classic spirit of the city was defined. Today, the Fremont Street Experience offers vis itors a chance to relive that golden era, with its vintage casinos, iconic lights, and a unique, nostalgic charm that sets it apart from the modern Strip.

As you wander beneath the dazzling canopy of lights that covers Fremont Street, you're immediately greeted by the unmistakable glow of classic neon signs that harken back to a different era of Las Vegas. The legendary **Vegas Vic**, the smiling cowboy who's been welcoming visitors since the 1950s, still stands tall, waving down from his perch above. The flashy marquees of vintage casinos like **Binion's**, **Golden Nugget**, and **El Cortez** invite you inside to experience the timeless thrill of slot machines, card tables, and the unmistakable energy that has defined Las Vegas for decades.

Fremont Street is where it all began—where the first casinos opened their doors, and where the spirit of Las Vegas took root. This historic center offers a glimpse into the city's past, contrasting sharply with the futuristic luxury of the Strip. The pace here is slower, the vibe more intimate, and the crowd more diverse. Instead of mega-resorts, you'll find smaller, iconic establishments, each with its own story to tell. Walking through Fremont feels like discovering a hidden treasure, where every corner reveals a piece of the city's storied history.

The street itself is an experience, with its famous **Viva Vision** light show lighting up the night sky in a stunning display of color and music. As the largest LED screen in the world, it stretches for five city blocks, creating an immersive spectacle that brings visitors together in awe. Below the canopy, street performers and artists fill the sidewalks, adding to the lively, carnival-like atmosphere. From musicians and magicians to living statues and acrobats, the performers of Fremont Street embody the playful, creative spirit of Las Vegas, inviting you to stop, watch, and be entertained.

Fremont Street also offers a unique contrast to the grandeur of the Strip. While the Strip is all about luxury and modernity, Fremont is the soul of *Vintage Vegas*, where the original charm of the city remains intact. It's a place where you can grab a drink at an old-school casino bar, try your luck at some of the oldest tables in town, or simply soak in the retro atmosphere that feels worlds away from the high-tech spectacle of Las Vegas Boulevard.

Whether you're visiting for a night out, a stroll down memory lane, or simply to experience a different side of the city, the Fremont Street Experience is a must-see for anyone wanting to feel the heartbeat of *Old Vegas*. Its vintage vibes and historic appeal make it a refreshing alternative to the Strip's nonstop energy, offering a nostalgic glimpse into the past while still providing plenty of excitement in the present.

The Fountains of Bellagio & Other Must-See Spots

No visit to Las Vegas is complete without experiencing the mesmerizing **Fountains of Bellagio**, a captivating blend of water, light, and music that has become one of the city's most iconic attractions. As you stand along the edge of the shimmering lake in front of the **Bellagio Hotel**, you'll be treated to a breathtaking display where water dances in perfect harmony to everything from classical masterpieces to modern hits. The fountains burst to life with jets of water shooting as high as 460 feet into the air, perfectly timed to the rhythm of the music and enhanced by brilliant lighting effects. The shows take place multiple times each day, and each one is unique, creating a magical experience that will leave you spellbound.

Just down the road, another must-see spectacle awaits at **The Mirage** with its fiery **Volcano**. This sensory explosion of fire, water, and sound erupts nightly, sending fireballs into the sky to the beat of a pulsating soundtrack. Watching the volcano spew molten lava and flames over the lagoon is an awe-inspiring experience, especially against the backdrop of the neon-lit night. It's a thrilling display that transports you to an exotic island paradise, if only for a few minutes.

For those who dream of drifting through the canals of Venice, **The Venetian's Gondola Rides** offer a charming escape from the desert. Hop aboard a sleek black gondola and glide under bridges and past colorful facades as your gondolier serenades you with traditional Italian songs. Whether you choose the indoor ride under the stunning blue sky-painted ceilings or the outdoor canal with views of the bustling Strip, this peaceful journey offers a romantic and whimsical break from the city's high energy.

As you continue to explore Las Vegas, one of the most striking visual experiences comes from looking skyward at the **Luxor**

Sky Beam. Shooting straight into the heavens from the top of the pyramid-shaped **Luxor Hotel**, this powerful beam of light is said to be the brightest in the world. Visible from miles away, the Luxor Sky Beam is a beacon in the desert night, a symbol of Las Vegas's ability to capture attention and imagination with sheer spectacle.

These iconic attractions are just a few of the many visual wonders that define Las Vegas. From the Bellagio's graceful fountains to the fiery eruption at The Mirage, from the tranquil gondola rides at The Venetian to the soaring Luxor light, these must-see spots offer unforgettable experiences that reflect the heart and soul of the city. Each one is a unique, artistic display of light, sound, and movement, promising to captivate your senses and transport you into the enchanting world of Las Vegas. Make sure to carve out time in your itinerary to witness these spectacular sights firsthand you won't want to miss them!

High Roller & SkyPod: Stunning Views of the City

For a view of Las Vegas that will take your breath away, look no further than the **High Roller** and the **SkyPod** at the STRAT two towering attractions that offer unforgettable, panoramic vistas of the city from dizzying heights.

The **High Roller**, standing at a towering 550 feet, is the largest observation wheel in the world. As you step into one of its spacious, air-conditioned cabins, you'll begin a serene 30-minute ride that slowly lifts you above the glimmering Strip, offering sweeping 360-degree views of Las Vegas and the surrounding desert. Whether you visit during the day to see the sprawling city basking in the sunlight or at night when the Strip is aglow with neon lights, the view is nothing short of spectacular. For those looking to add an extra element of fun, the High Roller offers a *happy hour* cabin, complete with an open bar. Sip on cocktails while taking in the sights—there's no better way to elevate your Vegas experience, literally!

If you're craving even more adrenaline, the **SkyPod** at the STRAT is the place to be. Perched atop the 1,149-foot **STRAT Tower**, the SkyPod delivers some of the most jaw-dropping views in all of Las Vegas. On a clear day, you can see as far as the surrounding mountains and desert landscapes, while at night, the sea of lights below transforms the city into a glittering spectacle. For the ultimate experience, head to the SkyPod around sunset to witness the desert sky's colors shift from warm pinks and oranges to deep blues, as the city begins to light up below.

Beyond the view, the SkyPod offers an extra dose of excitement for thrill-seekers. At the very top of the tower, you'll find a collection of *heart-pounding rides* like **Big Shot**, **X-Scream**, and **Insanity**—each designed to dangle you over the edge of the tower or shoot you into the sky, leaving your adrenaline pumping and your nerves racing. For those feeling especially daring, there's the **SkyJump**, a controlled free-fall jump from 829 feet high, making it the ultimate rush for adventure lovers.

Whether you choose the laid-back, luxurious ride of the High Roller or the sky-high thrills of the SkyPod, both attractions offer a unique perspective of Las Vegas. Each provides an exhilarating experience and a chance to see the city from a new angle whether you're marveling at the expansive daytime views or soaking in the dazzling nighttime cityscape. Don't miss the chance to rise above the action and enjoy these high-altitude adventures that will leave you with memories as impressive as the views themselves.

CHAPTER 3: THE ULTIMATE CASINO EXPERIENCE

Top Casinos: Where to Play, Bet, and Win Big

When it comes to gambling, Las Vegas reigns supreme, offering a thrilling array of top-tier casinos where you can play, bet, and (hopefully) win big. Each casino has its own unique atmosphere and gaming options that cater to all types of gamblers, from casual players to high-rollers.

At the **Bellagio**, elegance meets excitement. Known for its luxurious ambiance, the Bellagio is home to high-stakes poker rooms and an impressive collection of slot machines. The casino floor buzzes with anticipation, and its exclusive poker room has seen some of the world's greatest poker legends at the tables. With over 2,300 slot machines and a variety of table games like blackjack, baccarat, and roulette, this casino guarantees an unforgettable gaming experience amid opulence.

The **Venetian** offers an experience that blends gambling with old-world charm. Step into this Italian-inspired wonderland, where the casino floor sprawls with more than 120,000 square feet of gaming options, from popular slots to thrilling blackjack and roulette tables. What truly sets the Venetian apart is its inviting atmosphere and world-class service, offering a more laid-back vibe while still catering to high-stakes players in its exclusive poker room.

For those who crave excitement on a grand scale, the **MGM Grand** delivers in spades. This massive casino features one of the largest gaming floors in Las Vegas, with a staggering variety of slot machines, from penny slots to high-limit areas, and hundreds of table games. The MGM Grand's poker room is a favorite for tournament players, while its sportsbook is one of the best in town for betting on major sporting events. The sheer scale of this casino guarantees a thrilling time for every type of gambler.

From the grandeur of the Bellagio to the sprawling excitement of the MGM Grand, these top casinos promise the ultimate Las Vegas experience, where the next big win could be just around the corner.

Inside the World's Most Lavish Casinos

Step inside the world's most lavish casinos, where opulence, luxury, and elegance blend with the thrill of gaming to create an experience unlike any other. These palaces of entertainment are more than just places to gamble—they are destinations for those seeking the finest in comfort, service, and extravagance.

At the **Wynn Las Vegas**, you'll find a casino that embodies sophistication at every turn. The breathtaking design features towering ceilings, rich fabrics, and exquisite chandeliers, while the gaming floor boasts everything from high-limit slot machines to private poker rooms. Beyond gambling, guests can indulge in Wynn's high-end boutiques, Michelin-starred restaurants, and its award-winning spa, making it a world-class destination for luxury travelers.

Next, we enter the **Aria**, where modern elegance meets futuristic design. This sleek and contemporary casino is known for its cutting-edge gaming technology and sophisticated atmosphere. Aria offers high-limit lounges for serious players and a luxurious casino floor featuring thousands of slots and table games. Its upscale amenities extend beyond the gaming floor, with fine dining from celebrity chefs, posh cocktail bars, and exclusive VIP areas that cater to the most discerning guests.

At **The Cosmopolitan**, luxury and style are at the forefront. This casino's striking interior design is as impressive as its gaming offerings, with its mirrored columns, plush seating, and chandelier-draped bars. High-end gaming lounges, private rooms for the elite, and an extensive selection of both classic and modern games are all part of the experience. The Cosmopolitan's dining scene, rooftop pools, and luxury suites round out its status as one of Las Vegas's most glamorous destinations.

From the refined Wynn to the sleek Aria, Las Vegas's most lavish casinos offer more than just games—they provide an indulgent escape into a world of elegance, where luxury knows no bounds.

For the First-Time Gambler: Tips, Tricks & Etiquette

For first-time gamblers, stepping onto the casino floor in Las Vegas can be as exhilarating as it is overwhelming. But fear not this guide is here to help you navigate the world of gaming with confidence, providing useful tips, tricks, and etiquette for an enjoyable experience.

Start with a game that's easy to learn, like **slots**. Simply insert your money, press a button, and watch the reels spin. No strategy is required, and it's a great way to ease into the gaming atmosphere. For those looking for more interaction, **blackjack** is a beginner-friendly table game where you aim to get as close to 21 as possible without going over. Always remember: knowing the basic rules will improve your experience, so take a few minutes to study the game before you sit down.

Roulette is another classic, easy-to-follow game. Bet on a number, color, or section, and watch as the wheel spins. The odds are straightforward, and it offers a slower pace for new gamblers. For something a little more fast-paced, try **craps**. While the table may look intimidating, the basic bet—whether the shooter will roll a winning or losing number—is easy to understand.

A key part of gambling in Las Vegas is proper etiquette. Always be courteous to dealers and other players. If you're unsure about the rules of a game, don't hesitate to ask the dealer—they're there to help. Remember to tip your dealer and cocktail servers as a gesture of appreciation. Lastly, avoid over-committing financially: set a budget before you start, and never gamble more than you're willing to lose. The goal is to have fun, so play responsibly and enjoy the experience!

Budget-Friendly Gambling: Where to Try Your Luck

Las Vegas may be famous for its high-stakes tables, but you don't need to be a high roller to enjoy the thrill of gambling. For budget-conscious visitors, there are plenty of casinos that offer affordable gaming options, low table minimums, and generous slot payouts.

Downtown Las Vegas is a hotspot for budget-friendly gambling. Head to **El Cortez**, one of the oldest casinos in Vegas, where you'll find low table minimums and a vintage vibe. For those looking for even more bang for their buck, **The D Las Vegas** is known for its $5 blackjack tables and friendly atmosphere. The **Golden Nugget** also offers a classic casino experience with a variety of affordable gaming options and one of the best pools in the city to relax in after your games.

On the Strip, the **OYO Hotel & Casino** (formerly Hooters Casino) is famous for its lower-limit blackjack tables and value-friendly slots. **Treasure Island** is another great option for affordable table games, offering $5 blackjack and roulette tables alongside its extensive selection of slot machines.

To stretch your budget even further, make use of casino **loyalty programs**. Many casinos offer free membership cards that reward you with points for playing games, which can be redeemed for free meals, rooms, or even bonus play. Be sure to also check for **promotional offers** like free spins or match-play coupons.

With a bit of planning, you can experience the excitement of Las Vegas without breaking the bank. Whether you're spinning the reels or trying your hand at blackjack, these budget-friendly casinos offer a taste of the action at a fraction of the cost.

CHAPTER 4 ACCOMMODATIONS FOR EVERY TRAVELER

Luxury Resorts: Indulge in Five-Star Comfort

Las Vegas is home to some of the most extravagant and luxurious resorts in the world, each offering a unique blend of elegance, comfort, and indulgence. From lavish suites and world-class dining to opulent spas and exclusive gambling areas, these resorts promise an unparalleled experience for every traveler seeking the ultimate in luxury. Let's explore five of the finest five-star resorts in Las Vegas.

1. **Wynn Las Vegas**

- **Location: 3131 Las Vegas Boulevard South, Las Vegas, NV 89109**
- **Contact: +1 702-770-7000**

- **Website: Wynn Las Vegas**
- **Price Range: From $300 to $800 per night, depending on room type and season**

What it offers: A beacon of sophistication and glamour, **Wynn Las Vegas** is the epitome of luxury. The moment you enter its grand lobby, with its signature floral displays and serene atmosphere, you are immersed in an environment that exudes elegance. The rooms and suites are spacious, featuring floor-to-ceiling windows that offer stunning views of the Strip or the resort's immaculate gardens and pools. Plush furnishings, marble bathrooms, and cutting-edge technology create a sanctuary of comfort.

The **Wynn Spa** is an award-winning retreat where guests can indulge in a variety of treatments, from massages to facials, in a calming, beautifully designed space. Dining at the Wynn is an unforgettable experience, with restaurants like **SW Steakhouse**, where guests can enjoy world-class cuisine overlooking the enchanting Lake of Dreams. For those who enjoy a touch of exclusivity, Wynn's **high-limit gaming salons** provide an intimate, high-stakes gaming experience in a setting of refined elegance.

2. **Encore at Wynn Las Vegas**

- **Location: 3121 Las Vegas Boulevard South, Las Vegas, NV 89109**
- **Contact: +1 702-770-8000**
- **Website:** Encore at Wynn Las Vegas
- **Price Range: From $350 to $900 per night**

What it offers: Encore, the sister property to Wynn, offers an equally luxurious experience with a more modern, sophisticated twist. Guests are welcomed into a world of refined luxury, where the suites are expansive and feature contemporary designs, plush bedding, and state-of-the-art amenities. The **Encore Spa**, consistently ranked as one of the best in the world, offers luxurious treatments in a serene, upscale setting.

Dining at Encore is a journey through culinary excellence. **Sinatra** pays tribute to Frank Sinatra with Italian classics served in a nostalgic, upscale environment. For those who enjoy vibrant nightlife, **Encore Beach Club** provides a high-energy atmosphere with luxurious cabanas, stunning pools, and world-renowned DJs. The private **high-limit gaming rooms** at Encore offer an exclusive space for those seeking an elevated gambling experience.

3. **ARIA Resort & Casino**

- **Location: 3730 Las Vegas Boulevard South, Las Vegas, NV 89158**
- **Contact: +1 866-359-7757**
- **Website: ARIA Resort & Casino**
- **Price Range: From $250 to $700 per night**

What it offers: At ARIA Resort & Casino, modern luxury meets cutting-edge technology, creating a sophisticated and sleek environment. The rooms and suites are designed to blend style and comfort, featuri ng floor-to- ceiling windows and smart technology that tailors the room environment to your preferences. The **ARIA Sky Suites** offer a next-level experience with personal concierge services, private entrances, and exclusive amenities.

The **ARIA Spa & Salon** is a sanctuary of relaxation, offering unique treatments like hydrotherapy and a salt room, perfect for unwinding after a day of excitement. Dining at ARIA is extraordinary, with top-tier restaurants like **Jean Georges Steakhouse** and **Carbone** offering world-class cuisine. The casino at ARIA is vast, featuring a wide variety of games and high-limit rooms for those looking to gamble in style.

4. **The Cosmopolitan of Las Vegas**

- **Location: 3708 Las Vegas Boulevard South, Las Vegas, NV 89109**
- **Contact: +1 702-698-7000**
- **Website:** The Cosmopolitan of Las Vegas
- **Price Range: From $250 to $700 per night**

What it offers: The Cosmopolitan of Las Vegas is a resort that blends chic, contemporary design with bold, artistic flair. Known for its stylish interiors and creative touches, this resort offers a unique experience in the heart of the Strip. The rooms and suites are designed with modern elegance, many of which feature private terraces that offer breathtaking views of the city's skyline—a rarity in Las Vegas.

The **Sahra Spa & Hammam** is a luxurious, desert-inspired retreat where guests can experience a blend of ancient rituals and modern treatments. **The Chandelier**, a multi-level bar encased in thousands of crystals, is a must-visit for those seeking an exquisite cocktail experience. Dining at The Cosmopolitan is a culinary adventure, with a wide range of options, including **é by José Andrés**, a hidden gem that offers an intimate, avant-garde dining experience. The casino is vibrant and stylish, and the **high-limit gaming areas** cater to those looking for a more exclusive gambling environment.

5. **Bellagio Las Vegas**

- **Location: 3600 Las Vegas Boulevard South, Las Vegas, NV 89109**
- **Contact: +1 888-987-6667**
- **Website: Bellagio Las Vegas**
- **Price Range: From $300 to $800 per night**

What it offers: Perhaps the most iconic luxury resort in Las Vegas, **Bellagio** is known for its classic elegance and timeless beauty. Its Italian-inspired design is evident from the moment you enter the stunning lobby, home to the breathtaking **Fiori di Como** glass ceiling sculpture. The Bellagio's rooms and suites are luxurious and beautifully appointed, offering a mix of traditional and modern design elements, with stunning views of the famous **Bellagio Fountains** or the resort's lush gardens.

The **Bellagio Spa & Salon** provides a range of treatments in a tranquil, refined setting, perfect for relaxation after exploring the Strip. The Bellagio's dining options are renowned, featuring **Le Cirque** and **Picasso**, two restaurants that have earned Michelin stars for their exceptional cuisine. The **Bellagio**

Fountains are a must-see, offering daily water shows choreographed to music and lights, creating an enchanting atmosphere. The casino, with its high-limit poker rooms and exclusive salons, offers a sophisticated gaming experience that is second to none.

Budget-Friendly Hotels and Hidden Gem Stays

Las Vegas is famous for its luxury resorts, but that doesn't mean you have to break the bank to enjoy a comfortable stay. There are plenty of budget-friendly hotels and hidden gems throughout the city that offer fantastic value, great locations, and excellent service without compromising on quality. Whether you're seeking a cozy boutique hotel or a value resort with convenient access to the Strip, these accommodations provide all the essentials for a memorable stay—at a fraction of the cost.

1. **The D Las Vegas**

- **Location: 301 Fremont Street, Las Vegas, NV 89101**
- **Contact: +1 800-274-5825**
- **Website: The D Las Vegas**
- **Price: From $49 to $150 per night**

What it offers: Located in the heart of downtown Las Vegas, **The D** offers a lively atmosphere at an affordable price. This hotel combines classic Vegas vibes with modern amenities, featuring comfortable rooms, a vintage casino, and an exciting, high-energy ambiance. Its location on Fremont Street means you're steps away from the **Fremont Street Experience** and some of the city's best entertainment. Guests can enjoy lower table limits in the casino and a variety of casual dining options, making The D a favorite among budget-conscious travelers.

2. **Oasis at Gold Spike**

- **Location: 217 Las Vegas Blvd N, Las Vegas, NV 89101**
- **Contact: +1 702-768-9823**
- **Website:** Oasis at Gold Spike
- **Price: From $49 to $130 per night**

What it offers: For travelers seeking a boutique hotel experience, the **Oasis at Gold Spike** is a hidden gem in downtown Las Vegas. This chic, retro-inspired hotel offers trendy accommodations at an affordable rate. With a playful atmosphere, the hotel features unique amenities like an outdoor pool, backyard games, and a lively bar scene. Its central downtown location makes it perfect for exploring nearby attractions, while its modern design and hip vibe provide a stylish yet budget-friendly alternative to the big resorts.

3. **Circus Circus Hotel & Casino**

- **Location: 2880 Las Vegas Blvd S, Las Vegas, NV 89109**
- **Contact: +1 800-634-3450**
- **Website:** Circus Circus
- **Price: From $32 to $120 per night**

What it offers: If you're traveling with family or just looking for a fun, budget-friendly option on the Strip, **Circus Circus** is a great choice. Known for its carnival-like atmosphere, the hotel offers a wide range of affordable rooms and plenty of entertainment for all ages. Guests can enjoy the **Adventuredome**, an indoor theme park complete with rides and attractions, or catch one of the free circus shows performed daily. The hotel's convenient location at the northern end of the Strip makes it easy to explore the city without overspending on accommodations.

4. **El Cortez Hotel & Casino**

- **Location: 600 Fremont Street, Las Vegas, NV 89101**
- **Contact: +1 702-385-5200**
- **Website: El Cortez**
- **Price: From $38 to $150 per night**

What it offers: As one of the oldest hotels in Las Vegas, **El Cortez** is a downtown classic that offers great value and a charming, old-school Vegas experience. Recently renovated, this historic hotel combines vintage charm with modern conveniences, offering comfortable rooms and friendly service at an unbeatable price. El Cortez is located just steps from Fremont Street, making it an excellent option for travelers who want to be close to the action but prefer a more relaxed, low-key atmosphere than the Strip.

5. **Tuscany Suites & Casino**

- **Location: 255 E Flamingo Rd, Las Vegas, NV 89169**
- **Contact: +1 702-893-8933**
- **Website: Tuscany Suites & Casino**
- **Price: From $65 to $160 per night**

What it offers: Just a short walk from the Strip, **Tuscany Suites & Casino** offers spacious, suite-style accommodations at a budget-friendly price. Set in a quieter, more relaxed environment, this Mediterranean-inspired resort provides excellent value with its large rooms, outdoor pools, and on-site casino. Guests can enjoy easy access to the Strip while taking advantage of the resort's more laid-back vibe and lower prices. With its friendly staff, good location, and spacious suites, Tuscany Suites is a hidden gem for travelers seeking comfort on a budget.

These budget-friendly hotels and hidden gems prove that you don't need to sacrifice comfort or location to find an affordable stay in Las Vegas. Whether you're looking for a boutique hotel downtown or a value resort near the Strip, these options provide excellent accommodations, great service, and unbeatable value, making them perfect for travelers who want to experience the excitement of Las Vegas without the hefty price tag.

Alternative, Budget-Friendly Guesthouses In Las Vegas:

1. Sin City Hostel

- **Location**: 1208 Las Vegas Blvd S, Las Vegas, NV 89104

- **Contact**: +1 702-868-0222
- **Website**: Sin City Hostel
- **Price**: From $29- $35 per night
- **What it offers:** Perfect for backpackers and solo travelers, Sin City Hostel offers a friendly, social atmosphere with shared dorms and private rooms. It's located just a short distance from the Fremont Street Experience, offering easy access to Las Vegas nightlife and attractions. The hostel provides free breakfast, Wi-Fi, and a communal kitchen for guest use. With weekly events like BBQ nights and pub crawls, you'll have plenty of opportunities to meet fellow travelers. It's ideal for those looking for affordable yet comfortable accommodation in a prime location.

2. Traveler's Bed & Breakfast Hostel

- **Location**: 1502 S Las Vegas Blvd, Las Vegas, NV 89104
- **Contact**: +1 702-382-0450
- **Website**: Traveler's Bed & Breakfast
- **Price**: From $45 per night

- **What it offers:** Located near the Strip, Traveler's Bed & Breakfast Hostel is a budget-friendly option offering both shared dorms and private rooms. Each room is equipped with basic amenities such as air conditioning and Wi-Fi. Guests can enjoy free parking, laundry services, and a cozy common area. The hostel also provides easy access to nearby attractions like the Arts District and the Stratosphere. If you're looking for an affordable stay close to the action, this is a great choice.

3. Las Vegas Hostel

- **Location**: 1322 Fremont St, Las Vegas, NV 89101
- **Contact**: +1 702-385-1150
- **Website**: Las Vegas Hostel
- **Price**: From $25 per night
- **What it offers:** A vibrant hostel located near downtown Las Vegas, Las Vegas Hostel is perfect for budget-conscious travelers. Offeri ng dormitories and private rooms, the hostel provides amenities like a swimming pool, hot tub, free breakfast, and Wi-Fi. There's a communal kitchen and a cozy lounge area where guests can socialize. Its proximity to Fremont Street means

you're never far from entertainment. With friendly staff and regular events like karaoke nights, this hostel provides both comfort and a fun atmosphere.

4. Hostel Cat

- **Location**: 1236 S Las Vegas Blvd, Las Vegas, NV 89104
- **Contact**: +1 702-380-6902
- **Website**: Hostel Cat
- **Price**: From $30 per night
- **What it offers:** Known for its social and lively atmosphere, Hostel Cat is a great spot for solo travelers and groups looking to meet new people. The hostel offers both dorm-style and private rooms with essential amenities. Guests can enjoy free Wi-Fi, communal spaces, and organized events like pub crawls and group tours. Located just a short bus ride from the Strip, it provides easy access to the main attractions without the hefty price tag. It's an excellent choice for those wanting to explore Las Vegas on a budget.

5. Bungalows Hostel

- **Location**: 12301 1025 Fremont St, Las Vegas, NV 89101
- **Contact**: +1 702-998-7040
- **Website**: Bungalows Hostel
- **Price**: From $40 per night
- **What it offers:** Bungalows Hostel offers a quieter, more laid-back vibe compared to other options, making it ideal for those looking for a relaxing stay. It's located in the downtown area, close to Fremont Street. The hostel features shared and private accommodations with air conditioning and complimentary Wi-Fi. There's a fully equipped kitchen and a lounge area for guests to enjoy. This is a great spot for travelers wanting to be close to the action while still having a peaceful place to retreat to at night.

Family-Friendly Hotels & Kid-Approved Stays

While Las Vegas is often thought of as a playground for adults, it's also an exciting destination for families traveling with children. From hotels with sprawling pools and entertainment options to spacious family suites and childcare services, these family-friendly hotels are designed to ensure that everyone, from kids to parents, has a fun and comfortable stay. Whether you're looking for a hotel away from the casino crowds or one packed with kid-friendly activities, Las Vegas offers plenty of options perfect for families.

1. Mandalay Bay Resort and Casino

- **Location: 3950 Las Vegas Boulevard South, Las Vegas, NV 89119**
- **Contact: +1 877-632-7800**
- **Website: mandalaybay.com**
- **Price: From $150 per night**

What it offers: For families seeking a resort that doubles as a water wonderland, **Mandalay Bay** is a top choice. Its expansive **Mandalay Bay Beach** features a large wave pool, a lazy river, and over 2,700 tons of real sand, providing hours of fun for children and adults alike. The hotel also offers spacious family suites with plenty of room for everyone to spread out. **Shark Reef Aquarium**, located on-site, is a family favorite, allowing kids to explore marine life up close. Mandalay Bay's laid-back atmosphere, combined with its kid-friendly amenities, makes it a top pick for families visiting Las Vegas.

2. Circus Circus Hotel & Casino

- **Location: 2880 Las Vegas Boulevard South, Las Vegas, NV 89109**
- **Contact: +1 800-634-3450**
- **Website:** circuscircus.com
- **Price: From $55 per night**

What it offers: A classic for families, **Circus Circus** is packed with kid-approved entertainment. The **Adventuredome**, an indoor theme park with roller coasters, arcade games, and carnival-style attractions, will keep children entertained for hours. This iconic hotel also features daily circus performances, including acrobats, jugglers, and trapeze artists, all of which are free to guests. With affordable room rates, large family suites, and endless entertainment options for kids, Circus Circus is a budget-friendly option that never disappoints families.

3. Four Seasons Hotel Las Vegas

- **Location: 3960 Las Vegas Boulevard South, Las Vegas, NV 89119**

- **Contact: +1 702-632-5000**
- **Website: fourseasons.com**
- **Price: From $500 per night**

What it offers: For families looking to escape the casino atmosphere while still being close to the action, the **Four Seasons Hotel Las Vegas** offers an elegant, non-gaming retreat. Located on the upper floors of Mandalay Bay, this luxury hotel is known for its peaceful environment and world-class service. Families can enjoy the hotel's private pool, child-friendly dining options, and spacious suites. The Four Seasons also offers child care services and special amenities like kid-sized bathrobes, making it ideal for families who want a relaxing stay without the hustle and bustle of a casino.

4. The Mirage

- **Location: 3400 Las Vegas Boulevard South, Las Vegas, NV 89109**
- **Contact: +1 800-374-9000**
- **Website: mirage.com**
- **Price: From $130 per night**

What it offers: The Mirage is another great option for families, offering a range of activities and amenities that are perfect for kids. The hotel's famous **volcano** show, which erupts nightly, is a must-see for children of all ages. The Mirage also features a large pool area with waterfalls and lagoons, creating a tropical escape in the middle of the desert. Families can book connecting rooms or spacious suites, making it easy to accommodate larger groups. The Mirage's **Secret Garden and Dolphin Habitat**, where kids can see dolphins, lions, and tigers up close, is another highlight of this family-friendly hotel.

5. Hilton Grand Vacations on the Las Vegas Strip

- **Location: 2650 Las Vegas Boulevard South, Las Vegas, NV 89109**
- **Contact: +1 702-765-8300**
- **Website: hiltongrandvacations.com**
- **Price: From $200 per night**

What it offers: For families looking for a more residential feel, **Hilton Grand Vacations** offers spacious, apartment-style accommodations with fully equipped kitchens and separate living areas. Located at the northern end of the Strip, this non-gaming hotel provides a quieter, more family-oriented environment. The hotel features a kid-friendly pool, a game room, and a variety of activities like movie nights and crafts, ensuring there's always something fun for the little ones. With its family suites and home-like amenities, Hilton Grand Vacations is perfect for longer stays or families who want extra space and convenience.

These family-friendly hotels offer the perfect balance of comfort, fun, and convenience for guests of all ages. From water parks and theme park adventures to quiet, non-gaming retreats, these hotels are designed to make your family's stay in Las Vegas unforgettable. With plenty of kid-approved amenities and easy access to family-friendly attractions, these are the top places to ensure that everyone parents and kids alike has an amazing time.

CHAPTER 5: SPECTACULAR SHOWS & ENTERTAINMENT

Must-See Shows

Las Vegas is known for its jaw-dropping stage productions, and 2024-2025 promises an unforgettable lineup of must-see shows. At the heart of the Las Vegas entertainment scene is **Cirque du Soleil**, with several iconic performances that continue to mesmerize audiences. **"O"** at the Bellagio, featuring stunning water-based acrobatics, remains a fan favorite for its breathtaking blend of artistry and aquatic magic. **"KA"** at MGM Grand, with its cinematic martial arts battles and

rotating stage, offers an epic experience that leaves audiences in awe. Newcomers to the Cirque lineup include fresh productions that explore even more daring feats and artistic storytelling so be sure to watch for the latest shows making their mark in 2024 and beyond.

For magic lovers, Las Vegas is home to some of the most captivating illusionists in the world. **David Copperfield**, still performing at the MGM Grand, offers a masterful show of mind-bending illusions that defy explanation. For a more theatrical experience, **Criss Angel's Mindfreak** at Planet Hollywood combines rock concert energy with intense stunts and awe-inspiring illusions. Additionally, **Mat Franco**, the winner of *America's Got Talent*, continues to impress audiences at The LINQ with his interactive and personable style of magic.

From high-flying acrobatics to impossible illusions, these shows embody the magic of Las Vegas. Whether you're a fan of Cirque du Soleil's innovative performances or are drawn to world-class magicians, 2024-2025 will be packed with unforgettable stage productions that are an essential part of any Vegas trip.

Concerts, Stand-Up Comedy, & Variety Acts

Las Vegas offers an electrifying array of live entertainment options that go beyond the glitz of the Strip's main productions. Music lovers can catch legendary performances at venues like **The Colosseum at Caesars Palace**, where superstars such as

Celine Dion, **Adele**, and **Elton John** have performed iconic residencies. For 2024-2025, expect more top-tier talent with potential residencies from artists like **Usher**, **Katy Perry**, and **Bruno Mars**, as well as special concert events that will light up the city throughout the year.

If laughter is what you're after, Las Vegas has you covered with its robust stand-up comedy scene. The **Comedy Cellar** at The Rio brings New York's famous comedy club to Vegas, featuring big-name comedians and up-and-coming talent in an intimate setting. For a larger experience, head to **The Mirage** where top comedians like **Jerry Seinfeld**, **Jim Gaffigan**, and **Sebastian Maniscalco** are expected to grace the stage in 2024-2025. These comedy shows offer a hilarious escape and a great way to spend an evening in the city.

Variety acts also shine in Las Vegas, with shows that blend music, comedy, acrobatics, and dance. **Absinthe**, performed in a circus tent at Caesars Palace, combines raunchy humor with daredevil acts in a cabaret-style production that's unlike anything else in Vegas. Another hit, **The Blue Man Group** at the Luxor, offers a unique, high-energy performance that's equal parts music and visual spectacle. Whether you're after concerts, stand-up, or variety shows, Las Vegas has endless options for an entertaining night out.

Exclusive VIP Experiences & Backstage Passes

For those seeking to elevate their Las Vegas entertainment experience, exclusive VIP packages offer unparalleled access to the city's most famous shows. Imagine meeting your favorite performers, seeing behind the scenes of a major production, or enjoying premium seating with impeccable views—these are just some of the perks that come with a VIP ticket in Las Vegas.

Many Cirque du Soleil shows, including **"O"** and **"KA"**, offer VIP packages that include backstage tours, allowing guests to see the complex mechanics that power these jaw-dropping performances. Guests can explore the costumes, sets, and learn about the precision that goes into every show. **David Copperfield** also offers meet-and-greet opportunities, where fans can get up close with the master magician after witnessing his mind-boggling illusions.

For music lovers, **The Colosseum at Caesars Palace** and the **Park Theater** at Park MGM often provide premium seating packages that include early access, front-row seats, and post-show meet-and-greets with the artists. Many shows in Las Vegas also provide VIP lounges, where guests can relax in style before the show begins, with drinks and appetizers included.

Booking these VIP experiences is often done through the venue's website or concierge services, and tickets tend to sell out quickly for big-name performers. To make the most of your luxury outing, be sure to book early and plan to arrive at the venue in time to enjoy the full VIP experience. Whether it's a backstage tour or a front-row seat, these packages offer a one-of-a-kind way to enjoy Las Vegas entertainment.

Free Shows: Entertainment Without a Ticket

Las Vegas is known for its extravagant productions, but you don't need a ticket to enjoy some of the city's most captivating entertainment. The best free shows in Las Vegas bring excitement and spectacle to the streets, offering everyone a chance to experience the magic of the city.

The **Fountains of Bellagio** are one of the most iconic attractions in Las Vegas. This mesmerizing water show features over 1,200 fountains choreographed to music and lights, with water jets shooting as high as 460 feet in the air. Shows run every 30 minutes during the day and every 15 minutes at night. The best spot to view the fountains is directly in front of the Bellagio Hotel, where you can enjoy the stunning display against the backdrop of the city's neon lights.

Another must-see is the **Mirage Volcano**, which erupts nightly in a spectacular display of fire, water, and sound. This free show happens multiple times in the evening, and the best viewing spot is right in front of the Mirage, where you can feel the heat of the flames and experience the thrill of the eruption up close.

For a more interactive experience, head to **Fremont Street** in downtown Las Vegas, where street performers and live music acts create a vibrant, carnival-like atmosphere. **Viva Vision**, the largest LED screen in the world, lights up the night with music and visual displays that play above Fremont Street. Be sure to visit during one of their free concerts, where you can enjoy live music in one of the city's most iconic settings.

From the Bellagio Fountains to Fremont Street's nightly shows, these free attractions offer some of the best entertainment in Las Vegas without spending a dime. It's the perfect way to soak in the excitement of the city while saving your budget for other experiences.

CHAPTER 6: A CULINARY WONDERLAND

Celebrity Chef Restaurants: Where to Dine in Style

Gordon Ramsay Steak (Paris Las Vegas)

- *Ambiance*: Contemporary sophistication with a touch of French elegance.
- *Signature Dishes*: Beef Wellington, Sticky Toffee Pudding.
- *Experience*: Open kitchen adds an energetic vibe; perfect for fans of Ramsay's cuisine.

Giada (The Cromwell)

- *Ambiance*: Bright, airy space with floor-to-ceiling windows overlooking the Strip.

- *Signature Dishes*: Lemon Spaghetti, Marsala Herb Chicken Meatballs.
- *Experience*: A blend of Italian and Californian flavors with a welcoming, chic atmosphere.

CUT by Wolfgang Puck (The Venetian)

- *Ambiance*: Sleek and modern steakhouse with an upscale yet lively vibe.
- *Signature Dishes*: Australian Wagyu, Bone Marrow Flan.
- *Experience*: A high-end steakhouse experience with an extensive wine list.

Hidden Gems: Local Eats & Authentic Flavors

Tacos El Gordo

- *Location*: Off the Strip.
- *Specialty*: Authentic Mexican street tacos, especially Carne Asada and Al Pastor.
- *Experience*: No-frills, casual setting with consistently delicious tacos.

Lotus of Siam

- *Location*: Off the Strip in a shopping center.
- *Specialty*: Northern Thai dishes like Khao Soi and Crispy Duck Panang Curry.
- *Experience*: Family-owned, highly regarded by locals and food critics.

Eat. (Downtown Las Vegas)

- *Location*: Downtown.
- *Specialty*: Creative, locally sourced breakfast and brunch options like Truffled Egg Sandwiches and Shrimp & Grits.
- *Experience*: Cozy, casual atmosphere with fresh, made-from-scratch meals.

Buffets of Las Vegas: The Best All-You-Can-Eat Experiences

Bacchanal Buffet (Caesars Palace)

- *Cuisine*: 500+ dishes i ncluding fresh seafood, prime rib, and made-to-order pasta.

- *Standout Features*: Specialty nights with premium ingredients like Wagyu beef.
- *Experience*: Lavish, expansive buffet with a variety of global cuisines.

The Buffet at Wynn

- *Cuisine*: Upscale offerings including truffle-topped dishes, sushi, and rotisserie meats.
- *Standout Features*: Live cooking stations and a decadent dessert section.
- *Experience*: Elegant buffet with high-end dishes in a luxurious setting.

The Buffet at Bellagio

- *Cuisine*: International spread with seafood, caviar, sushi, and gourmet brunch items.
- *Standout Features*: Themed brunches featuring upscale ingredients.
- *Experience*: High-quality, diverse food offerings in a sophisticated environment.

Late-Night Dining: Satisfy Your Cravings After Hours

The Peppermill

- *Hours*: Open 24/7.
- *Cuisine*: Classic diner fare with oversized portions like pancakes, prime rib, and fruit plates.
- *Experience*: Retro atmosphere with neon-lit booths, perfect for a late-night bite.

Secret Pizza (The Cosmopolitan)

- *Hours*: Open late into the night.
- *Cuisine*: New York-style pizza by the slice.
- *Experience*: Hidden, no-si
- gn location makes it a fun and unique late-night stop for pizza lovers.

Grand Lux Café (The Venetian)

- *Hours*: Open 24/7.

- *Cuisine*: Wide-ranging menu from breakfast to comfort food like Steak and Eggs and Belgian Waffles.
- *Experience*: Upscale dining with casual comfort food options, ideal for late-night cravings.

CHAPTER 7: OUTDOOR ADVENTURES & DAY TRIPS

Red Rock Canyon: Hiking & Rock Climbing

Overview:

Just 17 miles west of Las Vegas, Red Rock Canyon offers stunning desert landscapes and is a top destination for outdoor enthusiasts. The area is known for its vibrant red rock formations, ideal for hiking and rock-climbing adventures.

Hiking Opportunities:

Scenic Trails: The 13-mile scenic drive provides access to several trailheads, offering a range of hikes that cater to all levels.

Easy:

Calico Basin Trail: A 2.2-mile loop with stunning red rock views, ideal for families and beginners.

Lost Creek Children's Discovery Trail: A short 0.7-mile hike leading to a seasonal waterfall, great for kids.

Moderate:

Calico Tanks Trail: A 2.5-mile round trip with moderate scrambling, rewarding hikers with a panoramic view of Las Vegas.

Challenging:

Ice Box Canyon Trail: A 2.6-mile trail with rocky terrain, leading to a seasonal waterfall—best for experienced hikers.

***Best Time to Visit*:**

- Spring (March to May) and Fall (September to November) are ideal for pleasant weather, while summer can be extremely hot.
- Early mornings or late afternoons offer cooler temperatures and fewer crowds.

Rock Climbing Opportunities:

Climbing Routes: Red Rock Canyon is famous for its world-class rock climbing, with over 2,000 routes available.

Beginner Climbers:

- *Panty Wall*: A great spot for beginners with shorter climbs and a variety of easy routes.

Intermediate to Advanced Climbers:

- *Solar Slab*: A popular multi-pitch route offering stunning views, perfect for more experienced climbers.
- *The Black Corridor*: A narrow canyon with various bolted sports routes, ideal for intermediate climbers.

Climbing Season:

- Best during cooler months (October to April) to avoid the intense summer heat.
- Winter offers good conditions, but mornings and late afternoons can be cold.

Tips for Adventurers:

Preparation:

- Bring plenty of water, sunscreen, and a hat as the desert sun can be harsh.
- Wear proper hiking or climbing shoes and layers, as temperatures can fluctuate.

For Climbers:

- Check local regulations and permits required for climbing.
- Beginners may consider hiring a guide for their first visit to ensure safety.

Red Rock Canyon is a must-visit for nature lovers and thrill-seekers alike. Whether you're hiking to enjoy the scenic beauty or tackling one of the many rock-climbing routes, this natural wonder offers something for everyone just a short drive from the Las Vegas Strip.

Hoover Dam & Lake Mead

Hoover Dam: An Engineering Marvel

***Overview*:**

Constructed during the Great Depression, the Hoover Dam is one of the most impressive engineering feats in American history. Standing at 726 feet tall and spanning the Colorado River between Nevada and Arizona, the dam not only generates hydroelectric power but also creates Lake Mead, the largest reservoir in the U.S.

***Visitor Tours*:**

- **Guided Tours**: Visitors can take guided tours of the dam, which include visits to the power plant and interior tunnels. The **Hoover Dam Powerplant Tour** and **Hoover Dam Tour** offer insights into the history, construction, and operation of the dam, providing a close-up look at this engineering wonder.

- **Visitor Center**: Stop by the **Hoover Dam Visitor Center** for interactive exhibits, historical displays, and breathtaking views of the dam and surrounding area.

Best Viewing Spots:

- **Mike O'Callaghan-Pat Tillman Memorial Bridge**: Offers stunning panoramic views of the dam and is a perfect spot for photography.
- **Top of the Dam**: Visitors can walk across the dam and take in the sweeping views of the Colorado River and Lake Mead.

Lake Mead: Recreation and Relaxation

Overview:

- Lake Mead, created by the Hoover Dam, is a haven for outdoor enthusiasts and offers an array of water-based activities. Spanning 112 miles, the lake is surrounded by rugged desert landscapes and provides plenty of opportunities for adventure and relaxation.

Activities:

- **Boating**: Rent a boat or take a guided tour of Lake Mead, exploring its clear waters and hidden coves. Marinas such as **Las Vegas Boat Harbor** and **Callville Bay** provide boat rentals, ranging from kayaks to houseboats.
- **Fishing**: Lake Mead is popular for bass, catfish, and trout fishing. There are several designated fishing spots, and visitors can either fish from the shore or rent a boat.
- **Water Sports**: Jet skiing, water skiing, paddleboarding, and swimming are all popular activities. The calm waters and warm temperatures make Lake Mead a favorite destination for water sports enthusiasts.
- **Hiking and Biking**: The nearby **Historic Railroad Hiking Trail** offers scenic views of Lake Mead and the Hoover Dam, perfect for those who prefer to explore on foot. The lake's shoreline also features trails for biking and hiking through the desert terrain.

Scenic Viewpoints & Picnic Spots

- **Boulder Beach**: A great spot for picnics and swimming, with beautiful views of the lake and plenty of shaded areas.

- **Hemenway Harbor**: Offers a scenic view of Lake Mead and is an ideal spot for a picnic while watching boats launch and return.
- **Willow Beach**: A quieter spot located on the Arizona side of the lake, perfect for picnics, kayaking, and enjoying the tranquil surroundings.
- **Overlook Points**: Throughout the Hoover Dam and Lake Mead area, multiple overlook points provide breathtaking views of the dam, lake, and desert landscape, perfect for photography and relaxation.

Best Times to Visit:

- Spring and Fall are the best seasons for outdoor activities due to the pleasant temperatures, while summer is ideal for water sports, although temperatures can be extremely hot. Winter is quieter but still offers beautiful scenery, especially for touring the dam and enjoying peaceful views of the lake.

Exploring Hoover Dam and Lake Mead offers a perfect blend of history, engineering marvels, and outdoor adventure. Whether you're fascinated by the architectural achievements of the dam or looking to enjoy the natural beauty and recreational opportunities of Lake Mead, this day trip promises something for everyone beyond the Las Vegas Strip.

The Grand Canyon: Tours

Overview:

The Grand Canyon is one of the world's most awe-inspiring natural wonders, and visiting it from Las Vegas is a popular day trip option. While the South Rim is the most famous section, the **West Rim** is the closest to Las Vegas, making it the most accessible for a day trip.

Day Trip Options:

Organized Day Tours:

- Many companies offer **guided day trips** to the Grand Canyon, with options for bus tours, helicopter rides, or airplane tours. These tours often include pickup from your hotel, meals, and scenic stops along the way.
- **Helicopter Tours**: These provide a breathtaking view of the canyon, with some tours even landing inside the canyon for an immersive experience. Helicopter tours typically include flyovers of the Hoover Dam and Lake Mead as well.
- **Bus Tours**: For a more affordable and relaxed experience, bus tours offer a guided journey through the Mojave Desert to the canyon, with stops at scenic

viewpoints. Many bus tours to the West Rim also include Skywalk tickets.

Self-Guided Trips:

- Renting a car and driving to the canyon is a great option for those who prefer flexibility. From Las Vegas, the West Rim is about a 2.5-hour drive, while the South Rim takes around 4.5 hours.
- Visitors can choose their own pace, stop at scenic spots along the way, and explore the Grand Canyon at their leisure.

West Rim vs. South Rim:

West Rim:

Distance: 2.5-hour drive from Las Vegas.

Key Attractions:

- **Grand Canyon Skywalk**: A glass bridge that extends out over the canyon, offering an exhilarating view of the Colorado River 4,000 feet below.
- **Helicopter Tours**: Some helicopter tours land at the canyon's base, allowing visitors to explore the Colorado River up close.

- *Experience*: The West Rim offers thrilling experiences and is more suitable for shorter day trips due to its proximity.

South Rim:

Distance: 4.5-hour drive from Las Vegas.

Key Attractions:

- **Mather Point**: One of the most iconic viewpoints, offering expansive views of the canyon's layered colors and depth.
- **Grand Canyon Village**: A historic area with shops, dining, and cultural exhibits, perfect for learning about the canyon's history and geology.
- *Experience*: The South Rim offers more hiking trails, viewpoints, and visitor amenities, making it ideal for those who want to immerse themselves in the natural beauty.

Tips for Making the Most of a Day Trip:

***Travel Times*:**

- West Rim: Plan for 5-6 hours round trip, with at least 3-4 hours at the canyon.
- South Rim: Plan for 9-10 hours round trip, allowing 3-5 hours to explore.

***What to Pack*:**

- Comfortable walking shoes, sunscreen, a hat, and sunglasses.
- Water and snacks, as the desert can get hot, and food options are limited at some stops.
- A camera or smartphone to capture the stunning views.
- A light jacket, as temperatures can vary significantly between the canyon's rims and base.

Whether you're seeking an adrenaline-filled experience at the Skywalk or a serene drive through the South Rim's stunning landscapes, a day trip to the Grand Canyon from Las Vegas offers a once-in-a-lifetime opportunity to explore one of the world's most iconic natural landmarks.

Thrills in the Desert

Dune Buggy Rides:

***Overview*:**

Dune buggy rides in the Las Vegas desert offer an exhilarating off-road adventure through the rugged terrain of dunes, dry riverbeds, and rocky trails. It's a thrilling way to experience the beauty and vastness of the Mojave Desert, providing an adrenaline rush while navigating challenging landscapes.

***What to Expect*:**

- **Terrain**: Expect a mix of soft dunes, winding trails, and open desert spaces perfect for high-speed driving. The terrain can be bumpy, with steep hills and sharp turns, making it a fun ride for those seeking excitement.
- **Duration**: Most dune buggy tours last between 1 to 3 hours, with options for longer rides that explore deeper into the desert. Some tours also include stops at scenic viewpoints or photo ops with the desert backdrop.

***Safety Tips*:**

- Wear protective gear, including helmets and goggles, provided by the tour operator.
- Listen to your guide's instructions, as the terrain can be unpredictable.
- Stay hydrated bring water, especially if riding during the hotter parts of the day.
- Dune buggy rides are generally suitable for all experience levels, as the guides ensure that riders feel comfortable and safe throughout the adventure.

***Booking*:**

- Tours can be booked through adventure companies in Las Vegas. Many offer hotel pick-up and drop-off services. Book in advance, especially during peak tourist seasons, to secure your spot.

Hot Air Ballooning:

***Overview*:**

- For a more serene yet equally thrilling experience, hot air ballooning offers a bird's-eye view of the sprawling desert landscape. Floating gently above the desert at sunrise or sunset provides a unique and peaceful perspective of the Mojave's beauty, with the ever-changing colors of the sky enhancing the experience.

***What to Expect*:**

- **Unique Perspective**: Hot air balloon rides give you a panoramic view of the desert, with sweeping vistas of dunes, mountain ranges, and even distant views of the Las Vegas Strip. At sunrise, the desert glows in hues of pink, orange, and red, creating a magical atmosphere.

- **Duration**: Most hot air balloon rides last about 1 to 1.5 hours, with the total experience (including inflation and deflation of the balloon) taking around 3 hours.

Safety Tips:

- Listen carefully to the pilot's safety briefing before takeoff.
- Dress in layers as the temperature can be cooler at higher altitudes, even if it's warm on the ground.
- Balloons typically operate in calm weather conditions, so expect potential rescheduling in case of strong winds.

Booking:

- Bookings can be made online through companies that specialize in hot air balloon tours. Since sunrise and sunset flights are the most popular, it's recommended to book early, particularly during peak seasons like spring and fall.

Whether you're speeding through the desert in a dune buggy or floating peacefully above it in a hot air balloon, these thrilling desert experiences near Las Vegas offer unforgettable adventures for thrill-seekers and nature lovers alike. Both activities highlight the natural beauty of the Mojave Desert while providing unique and exhilarating ways to explore its landscapes.

CHAPTER 8: GETTING AROUND LAS VEGAS

Transportation Options: From Taxis to Monorails

Getting around Las Vegas is easy and convenient, with a variety of transportation options catering to every traveler's needs. Whether you're navigating the bustling Strip, heading downtown, or venturing out for a day trip, here's a comprehensive guide to help you choose the best way to explore the city.

Taxis

- *Availability*: Taxis are widely available throughout Las Vegas, especially at major hotels, resorts, and the airport. You can easily find them queued outside the larger casino entrances or call for a pickup.
- *Cost*: Taxi fares typically start at around $3.50, with an additional $2.76 per mile, plus a $3 surcharge for airport

pickups. The average cost for a trip along the Strip is between $12 and $20, depending on traffic. Taxis are metered, so expect longer rides to increase the fare.

- *Convenience*: Taxis are ideal for point-to-point transportation, especially if you're traveling with luggage or want a direct route without navigating public transit. However, during peak hours or large events, taxi availability may be limited, and wait times could increase.

Rideshare Services (Uber & Lyft)

- *Availability*: Uber and Lyft are popular and widely available throughout Las Vegas, often providing a more affordable alternative to taxis. Rideshare pickups are available at designated areas in major hotels and the airport.
- *Cost*: Fares for Uber and Lyft are generally lower than taxis, with prices ranging from $8 to $15 for a ride along the Strip, depending on demand. Both services offer transparent pricing through their apps, so you'll know the fare upfront.
- *Convenience*: Rideshare services offer app-based bookings, making them a fast, efficient way to get around, especially if you're looking to avoid taxi lines. They also

provide various ride options, from budget-friendly UberX to more luxurious options like UberBLACK.

Las Vegas Monorail

- *Availability*: The **Las Vegas Monorail** runs along the east side of the Strip, connecting seven major stops, including MGM Grand, Paris/Bally's, and the Las Vegas Convention Center.
- *Cost*: Single-ride tickets cost $5, while unlimited day passes are available for $13. Multi-day passes offer savings for longer stays, with a 3-day pass priced at $29.
- *Convenience*: The monorail is a fast and reliable option, especially during peak times when road traffic can be slow. Trains run every 4-8 minutes, making it a convenient way to avoid the hustle of Strip traffic. However, it primarily services the east side of the Strip, so it may not be the best option for accessing attractions west of Las Vegas Boulevard.

Deuce and RTC Bus System

- *Availability*: The **Deuce** is a double-decker bus that runs 24/7 along the Strip, stopping at every major resort and attraction. The **RTC (Regional Transportation Commission)** bus system covers the Strip, downtown, and other parts of Las Vegas, including residential areas.

- *Cost*: A 2-hour pass costs $6, while a 24-hour pass is $8, and a 3-day pass is $20. These passes allow unlimited rides on both the Deuce and RTC buses.
- *Convenience*: Buses are a budget-friendly option for travelers looking to explore the Strip and downtown. The Deuce runs frequently, but it can get crowded during peak hours, and trips along the Strip may take longer due to traffic and frequent stops. The RTC system provides access to areas beyond the Strip, making it a good option for exploring the wider city.

Trams (Free Shuttle Services)

- *Availability*: Several free trams connect popular resorts along the Strip. The **Mandalay Bay – Excalibur Tram** stops at Mandalay Bay, Luxor, and Excalibur, while the **Aria Express Tram** links the Bellagio, Vdara, and Park MGM.
- *Cost*: Free of charge.
- *Convenience*: These trams are a convenient way to travel between hotels without the need to navigate traffic. They're particularly useful for shorter distances between adjacent resorts, allowing visitors to bypass the crowded streets.

Rental Cars

- *Availability*: Rental cars are widely available at McCarran International Airport and through major hotels and rental agencies across the city.
- *Cost*: Daily rental rates vary based on the type of vehicle and season, but budget rentals start around $30 per day. However, parking fees at some resorts can add to the cost, with charges ranging from $10 to $30 per day.
- *Convenience*: While rental cars offer the most flexibility for day trips outside of the city, such as to Red Rock Canyon or the Grand Canyon, they are less convenient for getting around the Strip due to traffic and parking fees. Visitors staying primarily on the Strip might prefer other transportation options.

Scooters and E-Bikes

- *Availability*: Electric scooters and bikes are available for rent through services like **Razor Share** or **RTC Bike Share**, with multiple pick-up and drop-off points along the Strip and downtown areas.
- *Cost*: E-bike rentals start around $5 for 30 minutes, with day passes available for $12. Scooter rentals may cost between $1 to unlock and $0.30 per minute.

- *Convenience*: Ideal for short-distance travel, scooters and e-bikes offer a fun and eco-friendly way to explore the city. However, they may not be practical for longer trips or during extremely hot weather.

Walking

- *Availability*: Walking is one of the most convenient ways to explore the Las Vegas Strip, especially since many resorts are located close to one another. Elevated pedestrian bridges provide safe crossings between hotels.
- *Cost*: Free, of course!
- *Convenience*: While walking is a great way to see the Strip, distances between resorts can be deceiving, and it can get hot during the day, especially in summer. Be prepared with comfortable shoes and stay hydrated.

Best Transportation Options Based on Needs

- **For Budget Travelers**: The **Deuce Bus** or **RTC buses** offer great value for exploring the Strip and downtown.
- **For Fast Access to Strip Attractions**: The **Monorail** is a convenient, traffic-free option.

- **For Flexibility and Convenience**: **Rideshare services** like Uber and Lyft provide on-demand transport across the city.
- **For Exploring Beyond the Strip**: Renting a car is ideal for trips to the Hoover Dam, Red Rock Canyon, or other nearby attractions.

Navigating Las Vegas is easy with these diverse transportation options, ensuring you can explore the city in a way that suits your budget, time, and travel preferences.

Renting a Car vs. Rideshare Apps: What to Know

When visiting Las Vegas, deciding between renting a car or relying on rideshare services like Uber and Lyft depends on your travel plans, budget, and how much you want to explore beyond the Strip. Here's a breakdown of the pros and cons for both options to help you make the best choice.

Renting a Car: Pros & Cons

Pros:

- **Flexibility**: Renting a car gives you full control over your schedule and destinations. This is especially beneficial if you plan to explore areas outside Las Vegas, such as Red Rock Canyon, the Hoover Dam, or the Grand Canyon.

- **Convenience for Day Trips**: If you're heading on a day trip to nearby attractions or national parks, renting a car is often the most convenient option.
- **Potentially Lower Costs for Long Distances**: For travelers visiting multiple off-Strip locations or staying in Las Vegas for an extended period, rental cars might be more cost-effective compared to rideshare fares for long distances.

Cons:

- **Parking Fees**: Many resorts on the Strip charge for parking, with fees ranging from $10 to $30 per day. These costs can add up quickly, making renting less economical if you're only staying on the Strip.
- **Traffic and Congestion**: The Strip can be notoriously congested, especially during weekends and events. Driving can be slow and stressful, particularly in high-traffic areas.
- **Limited Need for a Car on the Strip**: If your plans mostly involve exploring the Strip or downtown, you may find that a car is more of a hassle than a help, given the

walkability and availability of other transportation options like monorails and buses.

Rideshare Apps (Uber & Lyft): Pros & Cons

Pros:

- **Cost-Effective for Short Distances**: Uber and Lyft are typically more affordable than renting a car for short trips, especially if you're staying within the confines of the Strip or downtown Las Vegas. Average rideshare fares between Strip hotels are between $8 and $15.
- **No Parking Hassles**: With rideshare services, you avoid the headache of finding parking, paying parking fees, or navigating crowded parking garages.
- **Convenient Pickup and Drop-Off**: Designated rideshare pickup zones at most resorts make it easy to get a ride. Apps are easy to use and provide quick access to transportation without the need to wait for taxis.
- **No Need to Worry About Traffic**: While traffic on the Strip can still affect your rideshare, it's much less stressful when someone else is driving.

Cons:

- **Surge Pricing**: During peak hours, major events, or weekends, Uber and Lyft can implement surge pricing, meaning your fare could increase significantly.

- **Limited Availability During Peak Times**: When Las Vegas is busy, particularly after major shows or events, you may experience longer wait times for rideshare pickups.
- **Less Flexible for Day Trips**: If you're planning to explore beyond the Strip or downtown area, relying on rideshare apps can become more expensive and less convenient than renting a car for the day.

When to Rent a Car:

- **For Day Trips**: If you plan to visit attractions outside Las Vegas (e.g., Hoover Dam, Red Rock Canyon, Grand Canyon), renting a car is usually more convenient and cost-effective.
- **Exploring Off-Strip**: If your hotel is off the Strip or you want to visit lesser-known neighborhoods and attractions around the city, having a rental car offers more freedom.
- **Extended Stays**: If you're staying in Las Vegas for a longer period and plan on venturing beyond the Strip frequently, a rental car may be more economical.

When to Use Rideshare Apps:

- **Staying on the Strip**: If most of your trip revolves around exploring the Strip and nearby attractions, rideshare apps are more practical and less of a hassle than dealing with parking and traffic.
- **Short Trips**: For short, point-to-point trips—like hopping between casinos or heading to downtown Las Vegas—Uber and Lyft are often quicker and cheaper than renting a car.
- **Avoiding Parking Fees**: If you're staying at a hotel that charges high parking fees, using rideshare services can save you money and eliminate the stress of navigating Strip traffic.

Tips for Navigating Las Vegas Traffic & Parking:

- **Use Hotel Valet Services**: Many resorts offer valet parking for a slightly higher fee, which can be more convenient than self-parking. Some hotels even offer complimentary valet for hotel guests.
- **Check for Free Parking**: Some casinos and hotels, such as Wynn and Treasure Island, offer free parking. Be sure

to check the parking policies of your hotel or resort in advance.

- **Avoid Peak Traffic Times**: Las Vegas traffic tends to peak in the late afternoon and evening, especially on weekends. Plan your travel times accordingly to avoid congestion on the Strip.
- **Rideshare Pickup Locations**: Familiarize yourself with designated rideshare pickup areas at hotels and attractions, as these spots are often separate from regular taxi queues.

Renting a car is ideal for visitors planning to explore outside the Strip, while rideshare apps are more convenient for short, within-the-city travel. Consider your itinerary, budget, and preferences when deciding which option works best for your Las Vegas adventure.

Navigating the Strip: Walking, Scooters & More

The Las Vegas Strip is packed with iconic attractions, casinos, and entertainment, and there are several convenient ways to explore this famous boulevard. Whether you prefer to walk, rent a scooter, or use the free trams that connect major hotels, navigating the Strip can be both fun and efficient.

Walking the Strip

Pedestrian-Friendly Areas:

- Walking is one of the best ways to experience the Strip. Wide sidewalks, pedestrian bridges, and crosswalks make it easy to traverse the bustling boulevard.
- **Pedestrian Bridges**: Elevated bridges help you cross busy intersections safely, connecting key hotels like Bellagio, Caesars Palace, and The Venetian. These bridges provide easy access to attractions without waiting for traffic signals.
- **Key Points of Interest**: Many iconic spots, such as the **Fountains of Bellagio**, the **Eiffel Tower at Paris Las Vegas**, and the **Venetian Canals**, are easily accessible by foot. Walking allows you to take in the sights at your own pace, stop for photo opportunities, and soak up the vibrant atmosphere.

Tips for Walking:

- **Distance & Time**: The Strip is approximately 4.2 miles long, so while many attractions seem close, walking from one end to the other can take longer than expected. Plan your stops and break up your journey to avoid exhaustion.

- **Stay Hydrated**: Las Vegas can get hot, especially in summer, so carry water and wear sunscreen if you're walking during the day.
- **Comfortable Footwear**: With so much to explore, wearing comfortable shoes is crucial for enjoying your time on foot.

Renting Scooters

Availability:

- Electric scooters are available for rent throughout the Strip, often through services like **Razor Share** or **Scootaround**. These scooters can be found near major hotels and attractions, and they offer a fun and efficient way to navigate the area without walking long distances.

Cost:

- Scooter rental prices typically start at $1 to unlock and around $0.30 per minute, or you can rent by the hour or day. Some services offer discounted day passes for extended use.
- Scooters are a cost-effective way to explore the Strip, especially if you want to cover longer distances quickly.

Convenience & Safety:

- Scooters can be parked at designated spots, and many come with built-in GPS, making it easy to navigate. However, it's important to stay aware of pedestrian traffic and obey scooter riding laws, such as staying on designated paths and avoiding high-traffic areas.
- Always wear a helmet if available, and follow safety instructions to ensure a smooth ride.

Free Trams Connecting Hotels

Availability:

- Several free trams connect neighboring hotels on the Strip, making it easier to move between attractions without walking long distances or navigating traffic. These trams are perfect for saving time and energy, especially during hot days or when traveling between larger resorts.

Key Tram Routes:

- **Mandalay Bay – Excalibur Tram**: This tram stops at Mandalay Bay, Luxor, and Excalibur, providing easy access to the southern end of the Strip.

- **Aria Express Tram**: Running between Bellagio, Vdara, Park MGM, and Aria, this tram connects some of the most popular mid-Strip resorts.
- **The Mirage - Treasure Island Tram**: This tram connects The Mirage and Treasure Island, offering a quick ride between these attractions.

Convenience:

- Trams are a great option for bypassing traffic and getting from one major resort to another without additional costs. They're efficient, especially for guests staying at these hotels or those looking to explore multiple properties quickly.

Practical Tips for Exploring the Strip

- **Plan Your Route**: If you plan to visit multiple attractions, plan a route that minimizes backtracking. Use pedestrian bridges and trams to streamline your journey and reduce unnecessary walking.
- **Scooter Safety**: Stick to pedestrian-friendly areas and designated scooter paths. Avoid riding through heavily crowded areas, and be mindful of pedestrians and traffic rules.

- **Use Trams to Save Time**: When visiting resorts at the southern or mid-Strip, use the free trams to save time and energy, especially if you're covering longer distances.
- **Avoid Peak Hours**: The Strip can get extremely crowded during peak hours, particularly in the evening. Plan your travels accordingly to avoid the rush, especially if you're walking or using scooters.

Exploring the Strip on foot, by scooter, or via tram offers flexibility and ease, allowing you to fully immerse yourself in all that Las Vegas has to offer. By utilizing the various transportation options, you can navigate the Strip efficiently and enjoy all the iconic sights with minimal hassle.

Airport Transfers & Shuttle Services

McCarran International Airport (LAS) offers several convenient options for getting to and from your hotel or destination on the Las Vegas Strip, downtown, or beyond. Whether you're looking for cost-effective group transportation or luxury transfers, here's a comprehensive guide to the various airport transfer options available.

Shared Airport Shuttle Services

Overview:

- Shared shuttles are a budget-friendly option for individuals or small groups looking to get from the airport to their hotel. These shuttles operate regularly throughout the day and service most major hotels on the Strip and downtown.

Typical Fares:

- Prices for shared shuttles range from $10 to $15 per person, one way. Round-trip services are often available at a discounted rate.

Frequency:

- Shuttles generally run every 15 to 30 minutes, depending on the time of day and the company. They are available outside Terminals 1 and 3, with designated pickup spots for ease of use.

How to Book:

- Shuttles can be booked in advance online or upon arrival at the airport. Several operators, including **SuperShuttle** and **Bell Trans**, have kiosks near the baggage claim area for walk-up bookings.

- Pre-booking ensures you won't have to wait for the next available shuttle, especially during peak travel times.

Pros:

- Affordable and ideal for solo travelers or small groups.
- Convenient for those staying at major hotels, as shuttles drop off and pick up directly at hotel entrances.

Cons:

- Shuttles may make multiple stops at various hotels, which can extend travel time.
- Not as convenient for large groups or travelers who prefer private transportation.

Private Airport Shuttles

Overview:

For larger groups or travelers who prefer a direct, hassle-free transfer, private shuttle services are available. These offer door-to-door service without the need to share with other passengers.

Typical Fares:

- Private shuttles can range from $30 to $80, depending on the size of the vehicle and the distance to your hotel or destination.

- Round-trip options are available for those wanting to secure their return to the airport.

How to Book:

- Private shuttles can be booked online ahead of time, with operators like **Bell Trans** and **SuperShuttle** offering van, SUV, or luxury options to accommodate different group sizes.
- It's recommended to book in advance, especially for larger groups or during busy travel periods.

Pros:

- Direct service with no extra stops.
- Great for families, business travelers, or large groups wanting more privacy.
- Customizable options based on group size or desired level of comfort.

Ride-Sharing (Uber & Lyft)

Overview:

- Uber and Lyft are widely available at McCarran Airport, offering a convenient and affordable way to get to your hotel or destination.

- Dedicated rideshare pickup zones are located at Terminal 1 (Level 2 of the parking garage) and Terminal 3 (Valet level of the parking garage).

Typical Fares:

- A ride from the airport to the Strip usually costs between $12 and $20, depending on demand and your destination.
- Fares for downtown or off-strip hotels may vary but generally remain affordable.

How to Book:

- Simply use the Uber or Lyft app to request a ride after you've collected your luggage. Be sure to head to the designated pickup area, as rideshare vehicles cannot pick up curbside.

Pros:

- Affordable for individuals or small groups.
- Quick and convenient, with app-based bookings and real-time tracking.

Cons:

- Prices can increase significantly during surge pricing, especially during large events or peak times.

- May not be the best option for larger groups unless opting for UberXL or similar services.

Luxury Airport Transfers

Overview:

For those looking to arrive in style, several companies offer luxury airport transfers in private town cars, limousines, or even exotic vehicles.

Typical Fares:

- Prices for luxury transfers range from $60 to $150+, depending on the vehicle and level of service. Limousine rentals often include champagne and other amenities, making them perfect for special occasions.
- Many luxury services offer flat rates for airport pickups and drop-offs, which can be a good value for groups.

How to Book:

- Bookings can be made online in advance, with popular options including **Bell Limousine** and **Presidential Limousine**. Some high-end hotels also offer limousine services as part of their VIP packages.

Pros:

- Private, direct service with luxurious amenities.

- Great for special events, business travelers, or anyone looking to make a memorable first impression in Vegas.

Cons:

- Higher cost, not ideal for budget-conscious travelers.

Taxis

Overview:

- Taxis are a convenient and readily available option for airport transfers. Taxi stands are located outside both terminals, and you can typically hail a cab within minutes.

Typical Fares:

- Fares from the airport to the Strip range from $20 to $30, depending on traffic and your destination. There is also a $3 airport surcharge added to the fare.
- A ride to downtown Las Vegas will cost slightly more, around $30 to $40.

Pros:

- Quick and easy, especially if you prefer not to book in advance.
- Direct, no additional stops unless you request them.

Cons:

- More expensive than shared shuttles or rideshare services.
- Prices can fluctuate based on traffic, and some drivers may take longer routes to increase fares.

Cost-Effective Options

- **Shared Shuttles**: Best for budget travelers, with prices as low as $10 per person. Ideal for solo travelers or couples.
- **Rideshare (Uber/Lyft)**: Affordable and convenient, with rides between $12 and $20 to most Strip locations.
- **Taxis**: Slightly more expensive than rideshare services but readily available at the airport.

Luxury Options

- **Private Shuttles**: Perfect for groups or travelers looking for a direct and private experience without paying for full luxury services.
- **Limousines**: Ideal for those wanting a luxurious, memorable arrival with prices starting around $60 for town cars and $150+ for limousines.

Whether you're traveling solo, as part of a large group, or looking for a bit of luxury, McCarran International Airport offers a range of transportation options to suit your needs. By considering your budget, group size, and destination, you can easily find the best way to start your Las Vegas adventure.

CHAPTER 9: UNFORGETTABLE NIGHTLIFE

Best Nightclubs: Dance the Night Away

Las Vegas is home to some of the most exciting and electric nightclubs in the world, where visitors can experience unparalleled nightlife. From celebrity DJs and cutting-edge sound systems to extravagant light shows and opulent settings, these clubs are designed to provide unforgettable nights on the dance floor. Here's a guide to the top nightclubs in Las Vegas where you can dance the night away.

Omnia Nightclub (Caesars Palace)

Atmosphere:

- Omnia is one of the most stunning nightclubs in Las Vegas, known for its luxurious design and high-energy atmosphere. The club's centerpiece is a massive kinetic chandelier that moves to the beat of the music, creating a visual experience unlike any other.

- The rooftop terrace offers incredible views of the Strip, making it a great place to take a break from the dance floor.

Music & DJs:

- Omnia regularly features world-renowned DJs such as **Calvin Harris**, **Steve Aoki**, and **Zedd**, spinning a mix of EDM, house, and mainstream hits.
- The multi-level venue has different music genres on each floor, catering to a variety of tastes.

Crowd:

- Expect a trendy, upscale crowd, with a mix of locals, tourists, and celebrities. Omnia's lavish setting attracts a fashion-forward crowd looking to party in style.

Unique Features:

- The kinetic chandelier, combined with Omnia's state-of-the-art sound system and lighting, makes for a breathtaking audiovisual experience.
- VIP bottle service and private tables are available for those looking to elevate their night.

Hakkasan Nightclub (MGM Grand)

Atmosphere:

- Spanning five levels, Hakkasan is a mega-nightclub that combines luxury with high-energy nightlife. The club boasts multiple rooms and a sleek, modern design, making it one of the largest and most dynamic venues in Las Vegas.
- The Ling Ling Lounge on the third floor offers a more intimate vibe with hip-hop and open-format music, while the main room delivers a larger-than-life EDM experience.

Music & DJs:

- Hakkasan is known for its superstar DJ lineup, regularly hosting performances by **Tiësto**, **Martin Garrix**, and **The Chainsmokers**. The main room focuses on EDM and house music, with pulse-pounding beats keeping the energy high all night.
- Guests can also enjoy a variety of other music genres, including hip-hop and top 40 hits, in the club's multiple spaces.

Crowd:

- Hakkasan draws a diverse crowd of party-goers, from EDM enthusiasts to those looking for a more laid-back night in the lounge areas. The club's size and multi-level layout cater to a variety of tastes and experiences.

Unique Features:

- Hakkasan's innovative lighting system and immersive sound technology make it a sensory delight.
- The venue's multiple rooms allow guests to explore different environments and music genres, ensuring a unique experience every time you visit.

XS Nightclub (Wynn Las Vegas)

Atmosphere:

- Often regarded as one of the most luxurious nightclubs in the world, XS blends an opulent indoor space with an outdoor pool area, creating a unique, glamorous vibe. The gold-accented interior and expansive poolside cabanas provide an upscale party atmosphere that's hard to match.

- The outdoor area, complete with a pool and palm trees, is perfect for enjoying the desert night air while still being immersed in the energy of the club.

Music & DJs:

- XS features top-tier DJs like **David Guetta**, **Diplo**, and **Marshmello**, offering a mix of EDM, house, and electronic music.
- The music transitions seamlessly from the indoor dance floor to the outdoor pool area, ensuring that the party continues no matter where you are in the club.

Crowd:

- XS attracts a high-end crowd, including celebrities, VIPs, and those looking for an extravagant nightlife experience. The dress code is upscale, and bottle service is popular among guests who want to secure a private space for the night.

Unique Features:

- XS is known for its **Nightswim** events, where the party moves outdoors, and guests can dance poolside or even take a dip in the water.
- The combination of indoor and outdoor spaces creates a dynamic party environment, allowing guests to

transition between a lively dance floor and a relaxed, luxurious outdoor setting.

Marquee Nightclub (The Cosmopolitan)

Atmosphere:

- Marquee is a vibrant, multi-level nightclub that delivers a high-energy experience with its expansive dance floor and stunning rooftop terrace. The club's modern design, with LED displays and pulsing lights, creates an electric vibe throughout the night.
- The rooftop area offers sweeping views of the Las Vegas Strip and provides a more laid-back environment for those looking to take a break from dancing.

Music & DJs:

- Marquee regularly hosts A-list DJs like **Fisher**, **Dash Berlin**, and **Chris Lake**, with a focus on house, techno, and EDM. The energetic music and lighting effects ensure that the main room is always alive with energy.
- The rooftop terrace offers more diverse music, including hip-hop and open-format tracks, catering to different musical preferences.

Crowd:

- Marquee draws a stylish, young crowd looking for a high-energy party. The club's central location at The Cosmopolitan makes it a popular choice for both locals and tourists seeking a lively night out.

Unique Features:

- The **Rooftop Patio** offers a more intimate setting with stunning Strip views, providing a perfect balance to the high-octane main room.
- The club's multiple areas, including private booths and VIP tables, allow guests to customize their nightlife experience.

Drai's Nightclub (The Cromwell)

Atmosphere:

- Drai's is renowned for its rooftop location, offering unparalleled views of the Las Vegas skyline. The indoor/outdoor design features plush seating areas, luxurious cabanas, and a large dance floor that spills out onto the pool deck.

- The club's tropical ambiance, complete with palm trees and pools, makes for an unforgettable nightlife experience.

Music & DJs:

- Known for its live performances, Drai's focuses on hip-hop and R&B, with performances from artists like **Lil Wayne**, **2 Chainz**, and **Future**. This sets Drai's apart from other EDM-centric nightclubs on the Strip.
- DJs spin a mix of hip-hop, R&B, and top 40, ensuring that the music remains fresh and the dance floor stays packed.

Crowd:

- Drai's attracts a diverse crowd, including hip-hop lovers and those looking for a glamorous rooftop party. The dress code is upscale, with many guests opting for chic, stylish attire to match the club's luxurious setting.

Unique Features:

- The combination of a rooftop setting and live music performances gives Drai's a unique vibe, offering both a traditional nightclub experience and the excitement of a live concert.
- The pool area adds to the open-air feel, allowing guests to relax in cabanas or dance under the stars.

Rooftop Bars with Breathtaking Views

Las Vegas is not just about casinos and shows—its nightlife scene also includes a range of stunning rooftop bars that offer unforgettable views of the city's glittering skyline. Whether you're in the mood for a lively party atmosphere or a quiet, luxurious evening, these elevated lounges provide the perfect backdrop for a memorable night under the stars. Here are some of the best rooftop bars in Las Vegas that combine stunning vistas with great drinks and ambiance.

VooDoo Rooftop Nightclub (Rio All-Suite Hotel & Casino)

Ambiance:

Perched 51 stories above the Strip, **VooDoo Rooftop Nightclub** is the perfect combination of an outdoor bar and a lively nightclub. The open-air dance floor pulses with energy as DJs spin late into the night. Its laid-back early evening vibe transitions into a high-energy club scene, making it a versatile spot for both drinks and dancing.

Drinks:

VooDoo is known for its creative cocktails, most notably the **Witch Doctor** a monstrous rum-based drink served with dry ice for a mystical, smoky presentation.

The cocktail list is packed with tropical flavors and inventive presentations, sure to impress even seasoned cocktail enthusiasts.

Views:

With a 360-degree panoramic view of the Las Vegas Strip, downtown, and the surrounding desert, VooDoo offers one of the best vantage points in the city. The outdoor terrace gives guests the chance to marvel at the skyline while dancing under the stars or simply enjoying a cocktail at the bar.

SkyBar (Waldorf Astoria Las Vegas)

Ambiance:

Located on the 23rd floor of the luxurious Waldorf Astoria, **SkyBar** exudes sophistication and elegance. With floor-to-ceiling windows offering uninterrupted views of the Strip, SkyBar is a serene escape from the hustle and bustle below. The ambiance is calm and intimate, ideal for a romantic evening or a chic night out with friends.

Drinks:

SkyBar specializes in expertly crafted cocktails like the **Golden Hour**, a perfect blend of bourbon, apricot, and honey, evoking the warm glow of sunset. They also offer a carefully curated selection of fine wines, champagnes, and premium spirits.

Views:

The floor-to-ceiling windows and outdoor terrace provide unparalleled views of the Strip. Whether you visit at sunset or after dark, the city lights stretch out below, creating a magical, sparkling backdrop that's perfect for unwinding in style.

Legacy Club (Circa Resort & Casino)

Ambiance:

Inspired by the glamour of the 1920s, **Legacy Club** atop the Circa Resort is a nod to Vegas' golden age. With a rich, luxurious design featuring dark woods, gold accents, and a sleek outdoor terrace, the Legacy Club provides an upscale yet relaxed atmosphere.

Drinks:

The bar offers a premium selection of spirits, focusing on high-end whiskies and crafted cocktails. A standout is The **Gatsby**, a smooth bourbon cocktail with hints of blackberry and rosemary. For an even more elevated experience, bottle service is available for guests seeking to enjoy their drinks in true Vegas fashion.

Views:

From its perch atop Circa in downtown Las Vegas, the Legacy Club boasts stunning views of the Strip's skyline and the lively Fremont Street Experience below. The wraparound terrace offers a striking contrast between the modern Strip and vintage downtown, making it an ideal spot for watching the city transition from dusk to neon-lit night.

The Deck at Drai's Beachclub & Nightclub (The Cromwell)

Ambiance:

A mix of rooftop bars and high-energy nightclubs, **The Deck** at Drai's offers both daytime pool parties and nighttime revelry. By night, The Deck transforms into a vibrant outdoor space where you can dance, socialize, and enjoy world-class DJ performances under the stars.

Drinks:

The drink menu ranges from creative cocktails to premium bottle service. Whether you're enjoying a classic mojito or opting for a custom cocktail created by Drai's talented bartenders, the drinks here complement the energetic atmosphere.

Views:

Located on the rooftop of The Cromwell, Drai's offers breathtaking views of the Las Vegas Strip, including the iconic **Bellagio Fountains** and the nearby **Eiffel Tower at Paris Las Vegas**. The combination of a lively atmosphere and jaw-dropping views makes The Deck a must-visit for those looking to party with a view.

Skyfall Lounge (Delano Las Vegas)

Ambiance:

Sitting on the 64th floor of the Delano, **Skyfall Lounge** provides a chic, laid-back atmosphere with sleek, modern décor and cozy seating. The ambiance is intimate and relaxed, with DJ sets enhancing the energy as the evening progresses. It's the perfect spot for unwinding after a day of exploring the city.

Drinks:

The cocktail menu is eclectic and playful, featuring drinks like the **Noble Experiment**, a refreshing mezcal-based cocktail with hints of pineapple and jalapeño. Skyfall also offers a curated selection of craft beers and fine wines, ensuring there's something for everyone.

Views:

The expansive views from Skyfall Lounge are some of the best in Las Vegas. Guests are treated to sweeping vistas of the entire Strip and the surrounding desert landscape. Sunset is especially stunning here, with the sky transforming into shades of pink and orange before giving way to the glittering city lights below.

Dive Bars & Speakeasies

Las Vegas may be known for its glitzy nightclubs and lavish parties, but the city is also home to a thriving scene of dive bars and speakeasies that offer a more laid-back and intimate nightlife experience. These hidden gems are perfect for those looking to escape the hustle of the Strip and enjoy craft cocktails, unique decor, and a more local vibe. Here's a guide to the best dive bars and speakeasies in Las Vegas, capturing the city's hidden nightlife treasures after dark.

The Laundry Room (Downtown Las Vegas)

Ambiance:

Hidden inside **Commonwealth Bar** on Fremont Street, **The Laundry Room** is a classic speakeasy offering an intimate, vintage atmosphere.

With dim lighting, cozy seating, and 1920s-inspired decor, this spot feels like stepping back in time.

Drinks:

The cocktail menu is crafted to perfection, with bartenders creating bespoke drinks tailored to your preferences. Known for its attention to detail, The Laundry Room serves everything from classic cocktails to inventive creations, all prepared with precision and flair.

How to Find It:

Entry to The Laundry Room is by reservation only, and you'll need to send a text to secure a spot. Look for the unmarked door inside Commonwealth, and you'll be transported into a secret world of speakeasy charm.

The Griffin (Downtown Las Vegas)

Ambiance:

A true local favorite, **The Griffin** combines the gritty charm of a dive bar with an artsy, cozy vibe. The warm, dim lighting, complete with roaring fireplaces and a gothic aesthetic, creates a laid-back yet mysterious atmosphere. The crowd is typically a mix of locals, artists, and musicians, making it a great spot to experience the local scene.

Drinks:

Expect affordable drinks and a solid selection of craft beers, along with well-made cocktails. The Griffin offers a no-frills drink menu that pairs perfectly with the unpretentious vibe of the place.

Entertainment:

The Griffin frequently hosts live music and DJ sets in the back room, making it an ideal spot for catching up-and-coming local bands or grooving to indie and alternative tunes.

Velveteen Rabbit (Arts District)

Ambiance:

Tucked away in the Las Vegas **Arts District**, **Velveteen Rabbit** is an eclectic cocktail bar with a speakeasy vibe. The vintage, bohemian decor, with mismatched furniture and whimsical art, creates a cozy and welcoming atmosphere that feels worlds away from the flashy Strip.

Drinks:

Velveteen Rabbit is known for its craft cocktails, which change seasonally and are made with house-made syrups and fresh ingredients.

The bar's creative drinks often feature unique flavor combinations, ensuring every cocktail is an adventure.

Entertainment:

The bar regularly hosts themed nights, including trivia, karaoke, and live music, adding an extra layer of fun to the experience.

The Golden Tiki (Chinatown)

Ambiance:

Located in Chinatown, **The Golden Tiki** is a lively, immersive dive bar with a whimsical tiki theme. Filled with tropical decor, including glowing skulls, tiki idols, and animatronic parrots, the bar creates a fun and quirky atmosphere that feels like a hidden oasis in the desert.

Drinks:

As expected from a tiki bar, The Golden Tiki serves up exotic, rum-based cocktails like **Mai Tais**, **Zombies**, and **Painkillers**. The drinks are as playful as the decor, often served in elaborate mugs with colorful garnishes.

How to Find It:

Hidden in a nondescript strip mall, The Golden Tiki is a true hidden gem. Once inside, you'll be transported to a tropical paradise, making it worth the journey off the beaten path.

Frankie's Tiki Room (Off-Strip)

Ambiance:

An iconic dive bar with a retro Polynesian vibe, **Frankie's Tiki Room** is a local favorite for those in search of strong drinks and a laid-back atmosphere. The dimly lit space is filled with bamboo, tiki statues, and vintage tiki art, creating an authentic old-school vibe that's as charming as it is kitschy.

Drinks:

The menu is filled with classic tiki cocktails, many of which pack a serious punch. Try their signature drink, the **Fink Bomb**, for a blend of rum and tropical flavors. With potent concoctions and generous pours, Frankie's is known for getting the party started.

What to Expect:

Open 24/7, Frankie's is the perfect place to stop by any time of the night. With no pretension and no cover charge, it's a favorite dive bar for both locals and visitors looking to escape the glitz of the Strip.

Tips for Finding Dive Bars & Speakeasies in Las Vegas

Be Prepared to Search:

Many speakeasies are tucked away in unmarked locations, so be ready to look for hidden entrances, back alleys, or secret doors within larger venues. It's all part of the fun.

Reservations & Text Codes:

For exclusive speakeasies like The Laundry Room, making a reservation in advance is essential. Some venues even require texting a number to gain entry, so plan to secure your spot.

Dress for the Occasion:

Dive bars tend to be casual, while speakeasies might require a more polished look. Check dress codes in advance to avoid surprises at the door.

Where to Catch Live Music & DJ Sets

Las Vegas is a mecca for live music and DJ sets, with venues that cater to every musical taste, from rock and indie bands to world-renowned electronic dance music (EDM) DJs.

Whether you're a fan of intimate performances or grand spectacles, Las Vegas offers countless opportunities to experience unforgettable live performances. Here's a guide to the top venues where you can catch the best live music and DJ sets in the city.

House of Blues (Mandalay Bay)

Genres: Rock, Blues, Soul, and Indie.

Overview:

Located in **Mandalay Bay**, the **House of Blues** is one of the most iconic venues in Las Vegas, known for its intimate setting and diverse lineup of artists. The venue combines great acoustics with a lively atmosphere, making it a must-visit for music lovers.

Line-ups:

House of Blues regularly hosts a mix of national touring acts, indie artists, and even legendary performers like **Carlos Santana**, who has a residency here. The venue also offers themed nights, such as **Gospel Brunch**, where guests can enjoy live gospel music and Southern-inspired cuisine.

Ticketing Tips:

Tickets are generally affordable, but it's wise to book in advance for major artists or special performances. VIP seating is also available for an upgraded experience with better views and exclusive access.

Why Visit:

The intimate vibe and eclectic line-ups make this venue stand out, offering a chance to see both emerging and established artists in a smaller, up-close setting.

The Joint (Virgin Hotels Las Vegas)

Genres: Rock, Metal, Alternative, Pop.

Overview:

Formerly located at the Hard Rock Hotel, **The Joint** has moved to **Virgin Hotels Las Vegas**, but it still retains its reputation as one of the best places in the city to catch live rock shows. Known for its spacious yet intimate design, The Joint boasts excellent acoustics and often features big-name artists.

Line-ups:

The Joint has hosted legendary acts such as **Aerosmith**, **Guns N' Roses**, and **Imagine Dragons**. The venue is particularly known for bringing in major rock and metal bands, but it also features top pop and alternative artists.

Ticketing Tips:

Tickets for major acts can sell out quickly, so booking early is recommended. For the ultimate experience, look into VIP packages that often include meet-and-greets, exclusive merch, and premium seating.

Why Visit:

If you love rock and want to see some of the biggest names in the genre, The Joint is a must. The venue's impressive sound system and lighting enhance the experience, making it feel larger than life.

Omnia Nightclub (Caesars Palace)

Genres: Electronic Dance Music (EDM), House, Hip-Hop.

Overview:

Known for its high-energy atmosphere and top-tier DJs, **Omnia** is one of the premier spots for EDM fans in Las Vegas. With its massive main room, stunning visuals, and rotating chandelier that adds an electric ambiance, Omnia provides a nightclub experience unlike any other.

Line-ups:

Omnia regularly features some of the world's most famous DJs, including **Calvin Harris**, **Zedd**, and **Steve Aoki**. If you're a fan of electronic dance music, this is the place to be for non-stop beats and unforgettable performances.

Ticketing Tips:

It's highly recommended to buy tickets in advance, especially for popular DJ sets. Guest list options are available, and you can also opt for VIP bottle service if you're looking for an exclusive experience.

Why Visit:

The state-of-the-art sound system and the visual spectacle of Omnia's design make it a must-visit for EDM lovers. The energy here is contagious, making every set feel like a concert.

Brooklyn Bowl (The LINQ Promenade)

Genres: Rock, Indie, Funk, and DJ Sets.

Overview:

Brooklyn Bowl combines live music, bowling, and dining into one unique experience. It's an offbeat venue that brings a more casual, intimate vibe to live music, offering a mix of genres, from rock to funk and even DJ sets.

Line-ups:

Brooklyn Bowl hosts a variety of artists, from local indie bands to big-name performers like **The Roots** and **Jane's Addiction**. It's also a great spot for fans of funk and jam bands, with regular performances from well-known acts in these genres.

Ticketing Tips:

Tickets are reasonably priced, and the venue often offers deals for group bookings. Seating is first-come, first-served, but VIP options are available if you prefer a reserved spot.

Why Visit:

With its laid-back atmosphere, excellent food, and quirky bowling-lane setup, Brooklyn Bowl is perfect for a night out with friends or a more casual concert experience.

XS Nightclub (Encore at Wynn)

Genres: Electronic Dance Music (EDM).

Overview:

Known for its upscale, luxurious vibe, **XS Nightclub** at Encore is a premier venue for electronic dance music. With its elegant interior and massive outdoor pool area, XS offers an unmatched experience, combining a nightclub atmosphere with top-tier EDM performances.

Line-ups:

XS regularly brings in the biggest DJs in the world, including **David Guetta**, **The Chainsmokers**, and **Diplo**. The mix of indoor and outdoor space allows for an immersive music experience, with room to dance both indoors and by the pool.

Ticketing Tips:

Booking early is essential for popular DJ performances, as XS frequently sells out. VIP bottle service is also available for those looking to party in luxury.

Why Visit:

If you want to experience the height of Vegas nightlife with world-renowned DJs in a glamorous setting, XS is the place to be. The club's luxurious ambiance and cutting-edge sound system make it a standout on the Vegas EDM scene.

The Sand Dollar Lounge (Spring Mountain Road)

Genres: Blues, Rock, Jazz.

Overview:

The Sand Dollar Lounge is a legendary dive bar and live music venue, known for its intimate setting and history of hosting blues, jazz, and rock bands. A true hidden gem, this venue is beloved by locals and visitors alike for its laid-back vibe and incredible live music performances.

Line-ups:

The Sand Dollar Lounge features a rotating lineup of local talent, as well as regional and national touring blues and rock acts. You can expect everything from live blues jams to full-on rock performances, making it a go-to for live music purists.

Ticketing Tips:

No need to worry about expensive tickets here—the shows are typically free or low-cost, making it a budget-friendly option for music lovers.

Why Visit:

If you're seeking an authentic, off-strip experience with great live music in a cozy, unpretentious environment, The Sand

Dollar Lounge delivers. The relaxed setting and fantastic tunes make it a favorite for music fans looking to escape the more commercial Vegas venues.

CHAPTER 10: ART, CULTURE, & HISTORY

The Neon Museum & Mob Museum

Las Vegas is known for its glitz and glamour, but beyond the casinos, the city is rich in history, much of which is preserved in two of its most iconic museums: the **Neon Museum** and the **Mob Museum**. These museums offer a glimpse into the fascinating stories that shaped Las Vegas into the vibrant city it is today.

The Neon Museum

Overview:

The **Neon Museum**, also known as the "Neon Boneyard," is dedicated to collecting, preserving, and displaying iconic vintage signs from Las Vegas's past. This outdoor museum is a walk-through history, showcasing the signs that once lit up the Strip and downtown, many of which have become symbols of the city's unique character.

Exhibits:

Visitors can explore a vast collection of neon signs from classic hotels, casinos, and businesses, including iconic pieces like the **Stardust**, **Binion's Horseshoe**, and **Moulin Rouge** signs. Each sign tells a story, providing insight into the city's evolution from a desert outpost to the entertainment capital of the world.

Why Visit:

The Neon Museum offers a nostalgic trip through Las Vegas history and showcases the artistry behind these neon marvels. Guided tours provide historical context and fascinating anecdotes about the rise and fall of the landmarks these signs once represented. It's a must-visit for anyone interested in Las Vegas's colorful past and the unique role neon played in its identity.

The Mob Museum

Overview:

Located in a former federal courthouse, the **Mob Museum** (officially the National Museum of Organized Crime and Law Enforcement) offers an immersive look into the history of organized crime in the United States, with a particular focus on the mob's influence on Las Vegas.

Exhibits:

The museum features interactive exhibits and artifacts related to the Mafia's rise to power, infamous mob figures, and the efforts of law enforcement to bring them down. Highlights include the **St. Valentine's Day Massacre wall**, wiretapping devices, and courtroom exhibits where famous mob trials took place.

One of the museum's standout experiences is the **Prohibition exhibit**, which includes a fully operational speakeasy where visitors can enjoy authentic cocktails from the era.

Why Visit:

The Mob Museum brings to life the darker, lesser-known history of Las Vegas, showing how organized crime shaped the city's development. It's an intriguing and educational experience, with exhibits that delve into the real-life stories behind the city's glamorous façade.

Art & Installations

Las Vegas is home to a flourishing art scene that goes beyond the neon lights of the Strip. From massive public art installations to hidden gems in contemporary galleries, the city offers something for every art lover.

Public Installations & City Murals

Seven Magic Mountains:

Located just outside Las Vegas, **Seven Magic Mountains** is one of the most recognizable public art installations in the region. Created by Swiss artist **Ugo Rondinone**, this colorful stack of seven massive boulder towers stands tall in the desert landscape, offering a striking contrast to the natural surroundings. It's a must-see for anyone looking to experience large-scale, contemporary art.

Downtown Arts District Murals:

The **Downtown Las Vegas Arts District** is a haven for street art and murals. Strolling through this vibrant neighborhood, you'll discover dozens of murals painted by local and international artists, each telling a unique story. From large, bold designs to intricate, hidden gems, the murals reflect the creative energy of the community.

Fine Art Galleries

Marjorie Barrick Museum of Art (UNLV):

A hub for contemporary art in Las Vegas, the **Marjorie Barrick Museum** features rotating exhibits that highlight both local and international artists. The museum is known for showcasing diverse art forms, from installations and paintings to sculptures and video art.

Bellagio Gallery of Fine Art:

Located within the Bellagio Hotel, this gallery presents world-class exhibitions featuring works from some of the most renowned artists in history. Past exhibitions have included pieces from **Andy Warhol**, **Picasso**, and **Claude Monet**, making it a must-visit for lovers of classic and modern art.

Festivals & Community Events

Las Vegas offers a wide variety of cultural festivals and community events that celebrate the city's diversity and artistic spirit. From film festivals to art walks, there's always something happening beyond the casinos.

Las Vegas Film Festival

Overview:

Held annually, the **Las Vegas Film Festival** showcases a range of independent films, documentaries, and shorts from both local and international filmmakers. The event draws cinephiles and creators alike, offering screenings, panel discussions, and networking opportunities.

Why Visit:

This festival offers an exciting opportunity to engage with the film community and experience cutting-edge cinema in an intimate setting. Whether you're a filmmaker or a movie lover, the Las Vegas Film Festival offers a diverse selection of films that explore different perspectives and stories.

First Friday Art Walk

Overview:

The **First Friday Art Walk**, held in the Downtown Arts District, is a monthly event that celebrates local artists, musicians, and performers. Streets are lined with food trucks, vendors, and pop-up galleries, creating a vibrant festival atmosphere where the entire community comes together.

Why Visit:

First Friday is a fantastic way to experience the local art scene up close. Whether you're browsing the galleries or watching live performances, this community-driven event offers a great blend of creativity and culture.

Electric Daisy Carnival (EDC)

Overview:

One of the world's largest electronic dance music festivals, **EDC** takes place at the Las Vegas Motor Speedway each year. With massive stages, incredible light shows, and top EDM artists, EDC attracts hundreds of thousands of music lovers from around the globe.

Why Visit:

If you love electronic music and high-energy festivals, EDC is an unparalleled experience. The festival's immersive environment, with art installations and carnival rides, makes it more than just a concert—it's a sensory adventure.

Exploring Las Vegas Beyond the Strip

While the Strip often gets the spotlight, Las Vegas has diverse neighborhoods full of culture, art, and incredible food. Here's a guide to exploring the unique areas beyond the Strip.

Chinatown

Dining & Shopping:

Las Vegas's **Chinatown** is a hidden gem for food lovers, offering authentic Asian cuisine from various regions. Whether you're craving dim sum, ramen, or Korean barbecue, this district has a wealth of options. Popular spots include **Raku** (a Japanese izakaya) and **Pho Kim Long** for Vietnamese fare.

Cultural Experience:

Beyond the food, Chinatown is home to unique shopping experiences, including Asian supermarkets, specialty stores, and cultural shops offering everything from traditional tea sets to imported snacks.

Arts District

Art & Indie Shops:

The **Downtown Arts District** is the creative hub of Las Vegas, known for its vibrant murals, indie galleries, and eclectic boutiques. Wander through streets filled with vintage shops, tattoo parlors, and coffeehouses, and you'll get a feel for the local art scene.

Laid-Back Vibe:

Unlike the fast-paced Strip, the Arts District has a relaxed, bohemian atmosphere where you can stroll, shop, and take in the creativity of the community.

CHAPTER 11: DAY TRIPS & EXCURSIONS

A. Visiting the Hoover Dam & Lake Mead

A day trip to the **Hoover Dam** and **Lake Mead** is a perfect blend of history, engineering marvels, and outdoor recreation. Here's a comprehensive guide to help you make the most of this iconic experience.

Hoover Dam

History & Significance:

Completed in 1936 during the Great Depression, the Hoover Dam is a feat of engineering that tamed the Colorado River, providing water and power to much of the Southwest. At 726 feet tall and over 1,200 feet long, this concrete dam is a testament to human ingenuity. It holds back Lake Mead, the largest reservoir in the U.S., and provides hydroelectric power to Nevada, Arizona, and California.

What to Expect on a Tour:

Visitors can explore the dam on guided tours, which offer a behind-the-scenes look at its construction and operation. Highlights include walking through the tunnels inside the dam, viewing the massive generators in the power plant, and learning about the challenges faced by the workers who built it.

The **Visitor Center** offers exhibits and a film about the dam's history, and you can walk across the top of the dam, standing in two states at once Nevada and Arizona.

B. Lake Mead

Recreational Activities:

- **Boating**: Rent a boat or take a guided tour to explore the vast waters of Lake Mead. You can also try **kayaking** or **paddleboarding** in the quieter coves.
- **Hiking**: Numerous trails wind around the lake and surrounding desert, with the popular **Historic Railroad Trail** offering views of the lake and a walk through former railroad tunnels.
- **Fishing**: Lake Mead is a popular spot for fishing, with bass, catfish, and trout commonly caught in its waters.

Practical Tips for Your Day Trip:

- **Transportation**: The Hoover Dam is about a 45-minute drive from Las Vegas. You can either drive yourself or join one of the many guided tours that include round-trip transportation.
- **Dining**: While there are a few snack bars at the dam, nearby **Boulder City** offers a range of dining options, from casual cafes to sit-down restaurants.
- **Best Viewpoints**: For stunning photos, visit the **Mike O'Callaghan-Pat Tillman Memorial Bridge**, which provides panoramic views of the dam and the Colorado River. The top of the dam itself also offers great photo opportunities, especially at sunrise or sunset.

C. Explore the Grand Canyon

A trip to the **Grand Canyon** from Las Vegas is an awe-inspiring journey that offers visitors a chance to experience one of the world's most breathtaking natural wonders.

Ways to Explore

Guided Tours:

Many visitors opt for **guided bus tours** that depart from Las Vegas and take you to the **West Rim** or **South Rim** of the Grand Canyon. These tours often include stops at popular viewpoints like **Eagle Point**, **Guano Point**, and the **Skywalk** a glass bridge extending over the canyon's edge.

Helicopter Rides:

For an unforgettable experience, book a **helicopter tour** that offers aerial views of the canyon's towering cliffs and the Colorado River below. Some tours even land inside the canyon for a closer look.

Self-Drive:

If you prefer flexibility, rent a car and drive to the Grand Canyon. The **West Rim** is about 2.5 hours away, while the **South Rim** takes closer to 4.5 hours. This option allows you to explore the canyon at your own pace and discover lesser-known viewpoints.

Best Times to Visit

Spring and Fall are the ideal times to visit, with mild temperatures and fewer crowds. Summer can be hot, especially at the West Rim, while winter offers a quieter, more serene experience, particularly at the South Rim.

What to Bring

- **Comfortable Shoes**: Whether hiking or just walking along the viewpoints, sturdy shoes are a must.

- **Water and Snacks**: The desert heat can be intense, so staying hydrated is essential. Bring snacks or pack a picnic, as food options are limited in some areas.
- **Camera**: The Grand Canyon's views are unmatched, and you'll want to capture the stunning vistas from various viewpoints.

Must-See Viewpoints

- **Mather Point** (South Rim): One of the most iconic views of the canyon, perfect for sunrise and sunset photography.
- **Toroweap Overlook** (North Rim): A remote, lesser-known spot offering dramatic views without the crowds.
- **Skywalk** (West Rim): A glass bridge extending out over the canyon, offering a thrilling perspective for those brave enough to look down.

D. Excursions to Death Valley & Zion National Park

For those looking to experience two of the most diverse landscapes near Las Vegas, **Death Valley** and **Zion National Park** offer contrasting beauty that is easily reachable in a day.

Death Valley National Park

Overview:

Known as the hottest place on Earth, **Death Valley** is a surreal desert landscape of salt flats, dunes, and colorful badlands. Just a two-hour drive from Las Vegas, this park is a geologist's dream, with extreme temperatures and rugged terrain.

Highlights:

- **Badwater Basin**: The lowest point in North America, sitting 282 feet below sea level, with vast salt flats stretching as far as the eye can see.
- **Furnace Creek**: A popular spot for a rest stop, with the **Visitor Center** offering exhibits about the park's history and geology.
- **Zabriskie Point**: A stunning viewpoint where the colorful badlands meet the desert sky, perfect for sunrise or sunset.

Best Time to Visit:

Winter and spring are the best times to visit, as summer temperatures can soar above 120°F. Springtime brings wildflowers to the desert, adding vibrant color to the barren landscape.

Zion National Park

Overview:

Just under 3 hours from Las Vegas, **Zion National Park** is known for its towering red cliffs, scenic canyons, and lush valleys. It's a hiker's paradise, with trails for all levels of experience.

Highlights:

- **Angels Landing**: One of Zion's most famous hikes, offering panoramic views from the top of a steep, narrow ridge. Not for the faint of heart, but the view is worth the challenge.
- **The Narrows**: A unique hike through the Virgin River, where the canyon walls tower high above as you wade through the water.
- **Canyon Overlook**: A relatively easy hike leading to a spectacular viewpoint over Zion Canyon.

Best Time to Visit:

Spring and fall are ideal, with pleasant temperatures and fewer crowds. Summer can be hot, but the higher elevations of Zion offer some relief compared to the desert heat of Las Vegas.

Discovering Off-the-Grid Adventures

For the adventurous traveler, Las Vegas is surrounded by hidden gems waiting to be explored, far from the crowds and neon lights.

Ghost Towns

- **Rhyolite Ghost Town**: Located a bout 120 miles from Las Vegas, Rhyolite is one of the most well-preserved ghost towns in Nevada. Wander through the remnants of this once-bustling mining town, with its crumbling buildings and eerie atmosphere.

Desert Hiking

- **Valley of Fire State Park**: For those seeking solitude, Valley of Fire offers remote trails through red sandstone formations. Trails like **Fire Wave** and **White Domes** take you deep into the desert, where you'll often have the landscape to yourself.

Stargazing

- **Great Basin National Park**: One of the darkest skies in the country, Great Basin is a perfect spot for stargazing.

Far from city lights, the Milky Way lights up the night sky, offering an unparalleled view of the cosmos.

Practical Tips for Off-the-Grid Adventures

- **Safety First**: Always carry plenty of water, and a map, and let someone know your plans. Cell service may be limited in remote areas.
- **Pack for the Elements**: The desert can be harsh, with hot days and cold nights. Bring layers, sunscreen, and a hat for protection.

Exploring these off-the-grid locations offers a unique, more solitary experience of the Southwest, perfect for those seeking adventure and tranquility.

3-Day Itinerary

3-Day Itinerary: Highlights of Las Vegas

A 3-day trip to Las Vegas lets you experience the city's vibrant Strip, exciting entertainment, and nearby natural beauty, all while enjoying its world-renowned dining and nightlife.

Day 1: Explore the Strip and Iconic Hotels

• Start your day at the *Welcome to Fabulous Las Vegas* sign. Arrive early for great photos without the crowds.

• Head north along the Strip, visiting iconic hotels like *New York-New York*, where you can ride the Big Apple Coaster, or *Paris Las Vegas*, where you can take in the views from the Eiffel Tower replica.
• For lunch, stop by the *Venetian* and take a relaxing gondola ride along the indoor canals. Enjoy Italian cuisine at *Canaletto* or grab a casual bite at one of the many food spots along the *Grand Canal Shoppes*.
• In the afternoon, visit the *Bellagio*, famous for its Fountain Show and beautiful *Conservatory & Botanical Gardens*. Stay until evening to catch the mesmerizing fountain display, which runs every 30 minutes during the day and every 15 minutes after 8 p.m.
• For dinner, treat yourself to a meal at *Gordon Ramsay Steak* or *Giada*, both offering delicious fine dining experiences.

Day 2: Downtown Las Vegas and Fremont Street

• Begin your day by heading to *Downtown Las Vegas* and visit the *Neon Museum*, where you can see historic Vegas signs and learn about the city's unique history.
• For lunch, try *Pizza Rock* or *Carson Kitchen*, both highly recommended for their casual yet delicious food.
• In the afternoon, explore the *Mob Museum*, offering fascinating exhibits on organized crime in America.

• Spend the evening at the *Fremont Street Experience*, where you can zipline over the crowds on the *SlotZilla* or watch the light show on the *Viva Vision* canopy. Enjoy street performances and live music, and for dinner, visit *Le Thai* or *Oscar's Steakhouse* for a taste of local favorites.

Day 3: Natural Beauty and Adventure

• Take a break from the neon lights and drive to *Red Rock Canyon* for some hiking and breathtaking desert scenery. It's about a 30-minute drive from the Strip and offers plenty of short hikes or scenic drives if you prefer something less strenuous.
• Alternatively, book a tour to the *Hoover Dam*, located less than an hour from Vegas. The guided tours offer incredible views and insights into one of America's greatest engineering achievements.
• If you have more time, consider a full-day trip to the *Grand Canyon West Rim*, about a 2-hour drive from the city. The famous Skywalk offers stunning views 4,000 feet above the canyon floor.
• Return to Las Vegas in the evening and enjoy a farewell dinner at *Top of the World* at *The STRAT*, offering panoramic views of the city.

This 3-day itinerary provides a well-rounded experience of Las Vegas, from the excitement of the Strip and Fremont Street to the serene beauty of the surrounding natural wonders.

5-Day Itinerary:

A 5-day trip to Las Vegas offers the perfect mix of exploring the famous Strip, venturing into downtown's cultural spots, experiencing exciting entertainment, and taking day trips to natural wonders. Here's a detailed guide to help you make the most of your time in the city.

Day 1: Iconic Hotels and Shows on the Strip

- Start your adventure at the *Welcome to Fabulous Las Vegas* sign for a classic photo op.
- Spend your morning walking along the Strip, stopping at *Caesars Palace, Paris Las Vegas,* and *Bellagio.*
- For lunch, try *Mon Ami Gabi* at *Paris Las Vegas* or grab a casual meal at *Gordon Ramsay Fish & Chips* at *The LINQ.*
- In the afternoon, take a gondola ride at *The Venetian* or visit the *High Roller* at *The LINQ Promenade* for a bird's-eye view of the city.
- Wrap up your day with dinner and a world-class show. Consider *Absinthe* at *Caesars Palace* for an entertaining mix of comedy and circus-style performances.

Day 2: Museums and Culture in Downtown Las Vegas

• Head to *Downtown Las Vegas* and visit the *Neon Museum* to explore vintage Vegas signs.
• Next, immerse yourself in history at the *Mob Museum*, which offers fascinating exhibits on organized crime in the U.S.
• Have lunch at *Pizza Rock* or *Eat*, a favorite among locals.
• Spend the evening exploring the *Fremont Street Experience*, where you can zipline, people-watch, and enjoy live music and street performances. Don't miss the dazzling Viva Vision light show, which runs hourly after dark.
• For dinner, enjoy a meal at *Le Thai* or *Oscar's Steakhouse.*

Day 3: Day Trip to Hoover Dam and Red Rock Canyon

• Take a break from the hustle and bustle with a day trip to the *Hoover Dam*. The drive is less than an hour from Vegas, and tours offer a deep dive into this engineering marvel.
• On your way back, stop at *Red Rock Canyon* for a scenic hike or a leisurely drive through its stunning rock formations.
• Return to Vegas in the evening and unwind with dinner at *Top of the World* at *The STRAT*, offering incredible 360-degree views of the city.

Day 4: Shopping and Relaxation

• Spend the morning exploring the *Fashion Show Mall* or browsing luxury shops at *The Forum Shops at Caesars.*
• For lunch, head to *Bacchanal Buffet* at *Caesars Palace,* which is renowned for its vast selection of gourmet dishes.
• In the afternoon, relax by the pool at your hotel, or treat yourself to a spa day at *Qua Baths & Spa* at *Caesars Palace.*
• In the evening, enjoy a casual dinner at *Ellis Island* for a classic Vegas steak dinner or explore the many dining options at *The Cosmopolitan.* Wrap up your night with cocktails at a hidden speakeasy-like *Ghost Donkey.*

Day 5: Adventure and Departure

• On your last day, take a trip to the *Seven Magic Mountains,* a colorful art installation in the desert just 25 minutes from the city. It's a fun and quick trip, perfect for unique photos.
• For lunch, head to *Peppermill,* a Vegas classic, or *In-N-Out Burger* for a quick, casual meal.
• Spend your final afternoon revisiting any favorite spots on the Strip, like the *Bellagio Fountains* or the *Venetian Canals,* before heading to the airport. If time allows, enjoy one last relaxing poolside cocktail

7-Day Itinerary:

A 7-day trip to Las Vegas lets you fully immerse yourself in the city's attractions, from its world-famous Strip and vibrant nightlife to its natural wonders and hidden gems. With this itinerary, you'll explore all the must-see landmarks, enjoy exciting day trips, and experience Las Vegas like never before.

Day 1: Welcome to the Strip

• Start your journey at the *Welcome to Fabulous Las Vegas* sign for an iconic photo.

• Take a leisurely walk down the Strip, visiting some of Vegas' most famous hotels: *Bellagio, Caesars Palace,* and *Paris Las Vegas.* Don't miss the *Bellagio Fountain Show* and the beautiful *Conservatory & Botanical Gardens.*

• For lunch, try *Gordon Ramsay Burger* at *Planet Hollywood,* or grab a bite at *Mon Ami Gabi* for stunning views of the Strip.

• End your first day with a world-class show like *Cirque du Soleil* at the *Mirage* or *Absinthe* at *Caesars Palace.*

Day 2: Explore Downtown and Fremont Street

• Head to *Downtown Las Vegas* and explore the *Mob Museum* to learn about the city's history with organized crime.

• Grab lunch at *Pizza Rock* or *Le Thai*, both local favorites.

• In the afternoon, visit the *Neon Museum*, where vintage Vegas signs are displayed in an outdoor gallery.

• Spend your evening at the *Fremont Street Experience*, where you can zipline on the *SlotZilla*, enjoy street performances, and catch the dazzling *Viva Vision* light show.

Day 3: Adventure to Red Rock Canyon and Hoover Dam

• Escape the city with a morning trip to *Red Rock Canyon*. Just 30 minutes from the Strip, this natural wonder offers scenic hiking trails and picturesque views. • Afterward, head to the *Hoover Dam* for a guided tour of this engineering marvel. • Return to the city in the evening and enjoy dinner at *Top of the World* at *The STRAT*, where you'll get panoramic views of the city

Day 4: Arts District and Local Culture

• Start your day with a hearty breakfast at *Vickie's Diner*, a retro, all-pink 1950s-themed diner. • Explore the *Las Vegas Arts District*, where you'll find galleries, vintage shops, and unique street art. Don't miss local breweries like *Able Baker Brewing* or *Hop Nuts Brewing* for a refreshing afternoon drink. • After lunch, visit the *Pinball Hall of Fame*, packed with retro arcade games. •

For dinner, check out *The Peppermill*, a Vegas classic known for its vintage vibe and large portions.

Day 5: Day Trip to the Grand Canyon or Valley of Fire

• Take a full-day trip to the *Grand Canyon West Rim*. Explore the *Skywalk*, a glass bridge 4,000 feet above the canyon floor, for incredible views. Alternatively, visit the *Valley of Fire State Park*, known for its striking red rock formations and petroglyphs. • Upon your return, relax with dinner at *The Cosmopolitan's Wicked Spoon* buffet.

Day 6: Shopping and Relaxation

• Spend the morning shopping at the *Fashion Show Mall* or *The Forum Shops at Caesars*, which feature luxury brands and a unique Roman-themed atmosphere. • Afterward, enjoy a relaxing spa day at *Qua Baths & Spa* at *Caesars Palace* or at *Sahra Spa* at *The Cosmopolitan*. • For dinner, try *Nobu* at *Caesars Palace* or *Momofuku* at *The Cosmopolitan*, two highly recommended fine-dining options.

Day 7: Hidden Gems and Departure

• Visit *Seven Magic Mountains*, a colorful art installation in the desert, just 25 minutes from Las Vegas. It's the perfect spot for unique photos. • For lunch, stop by *In-N-Out Burger* or grab brunch at *The Henry* at *The Cosmopolitan.* • Spend your final afternoon relaxing by your hotel pool or revisiting any favorite spots along the Strip before your departure.

This 7-day itinerary offers the perfect blend of excitement, adventure, relaxation, and cultural experiences, ensuring you see the best of Las Vegas and its surrounding areas. From iconic landmarks to day trips and hidden gems, you'll leave with unforgettable memories of your trip to Sin City.

CHAPTER 12: PRACTICAL INFORMATION FOR FIRST-TIME VISITORS

Best Times to Visit Las Vegas

When planning a trip to Las Vegas, timing is everything. The city's energy pulses year-round, but certain seasons offer distinct advantages based on your preferences for weather, crowds, and special events. Here's a breakdown of what to expect in each season to help you pick the perfect time to visit.

Spring (March to May)

Weather:

Spring is one of the best times to visit Las Vegas, with daytime temperatures ranging from 60°F to 85°F. The weather is pleasant, making it ideal for walking the Strip and enjoying outdoor activities like hiking at Red Rock Canyon.

Crowd Levels:

As the weather is perfect for outdoor exploration, crowds begin to pick up, especially during spring break and major events. March Madness brings in sports fans, while music festivals and conventions draw larger crowds in April and May.

Special Events:

Popular events like **NASCAR races**, the **NHL playoffs**, and the **Viva Las Vegas Rockabilly Weekend** take place during this time. These events can make for an exciting trip but also mean increased hotel prices.

Summer (June to August)

Weather:

Summers in Las Vegas are scorching, with temperatures often exceeding 100°F. Expect hot, dry days and balmy evenings, which makes spending time by the pool or in air-conditioned casinos essential.

Crowd Levels:

Despite the heat, Las Vegas is packed with tourists during the summer, especially in June and July. This is prime vacation season for families and international travelers.

Special Events:

4th of July celebrations and pool parties at major hotels like **Wet Republic** and **Drai's Beachclub** are the highlights of the summer. **EDC Las Vegas** also brings in large crowds in May or June. Be prepared for packed venues and higher rates for flights and hotels during these times.

Fall (September to November)

Weather:

Fall is another prime time to visit, with temperatures cooling down to a more manageable range of 60°F to 90°F. It's great weather for exploring the Strip, enjoying outdoor attractions, or taking day trips to nearby destinations like the Grand Canyon.

Crowd Levels:

September is still busy due to Labor Day, but as fall progresses, the crowds thin out, especially in October and November. Hotel prices are more reasonable during this time.

Special Events:

Popular events in the fall include the **Life is Beautiful Festival** in September and **Las Vegas Pride** in October. November hosts major conventions like the **SEMA Show** and **Automotive**

Aftermarket Expo, which can impact hotel availability and prices.

Winter (December to February)

Weather:

Winter brings cooler temperatures, ranging from 40°F to 60°F, but rarely freezing. It's still comfortable enough to walk the Strip, but you'll want to bring layers for the chilly evenings.

Crowd Levels:

December sees a spike in visitors around **New Year's Eve**, one of the busiest and most expensive times to visit. January and February are quieter months, making it a great time for travelers seeking fewer crowds and better deals on hotels.

Special Events:

The **National Finals Rodeo** takes place in December, and the city is packed for New Year's Eve celebrations. In February, there are Super Bowl parties and the **CES technology convention**, both of which draw large crowds.

Packing Essentials & What to Expect

Las Vegas is a unique destination, and packing the right items can make your trip smoother and more enjoyable. Here's a practical guide to help you pack for both the day and night, as well as what to expect upon arrival.

Clothing Recommendations

Daytime:

- Depending on the season, you'll need lightweight, breathable clothing for hot summer days or layers for cooler months. Casual attire is fine for most daytime activities.
- Comfortable walking shoes are a must! The Strip is much longer than it looks, and you'll be doing a lot of walking between hotels, casinos, and attractions.

Evening:

Many restaurants, nightclubs, and shows have dress codes. If you plan to hit the nightlife scene, bring upscale attire. Men should pack a button-down shirt and nice shoes, while women might opt for a cocktail dress or stylish outfit.

Essential Items

Sunscreen & Sunglasses:

The desert sun can be harsh, even in winter. Protect your skin with sunscreen and bring sunglasses for walking during the day.

Reusable Water Bottle:

Staying hydrated is crucial, especially if you're visiting in the summer or plan to spend time outdoors. Hotels typically provide water refill stations, and bringing your own bottle will save money.

Portable Phone Charger:

With all the walking and photo-taking, your phone's battery might drain faster than usual. A portable charger will ensure you don't run out of power.

What to Expect

Weather Conditions:

Las Vegas can have extreme weather, with scorching summers and cooler winters, so packing appropriately for the season is essential. The climate is very dry, so moisturizing lotion is recommended to combat dry skin.

Typical Experiences:

Visitors should expect long distances between attractions on the Strip, as well as the need for comfortable shoes. Most of the excitement in Las Vegas happens at night, from shows and dining to casinos and clubs, so plan for late nights.

Casinos & Indoor Spaces:

Casinos allow smoking, so if you're sensitive to smoke, keep that in mind for indoor spaces. Most hotels are large and can take a while to navigate, so give yourself plenty of time to get to shows or restaurants.

Navigating Las Vegas: Tips for First-Time Travelers

Getting around Las Vegas can be tricky, especially for first-time visitors. Here's a breakdown of the best ways to move around the city, ensuring you don't waste time or overspend.

Walking the Strip

Distances:

The Las Vegas Strip is over 4 miles long, and while walking between major hotels might seem easy, distances can be deceiving. Expect to walk a lot and allow more time than you think to get from one point to another.

Pedestrian-Friendly:

Pedestrian bridges and wide sidewalks make walking relatively easy, but the heat can be intense, especially in summer, so plan breaks and stay hydrated.

Monorail & Public Transit

Las Vegas Monorail:

- The monorail runs along the east side of the Strip, connecting popular hotels like MGM Grand, Bally's, and the Las Vegas Convention Center. It's fast and avoids traffic, making it a convenient option for moving between major attractions.
- Tickets cost $5 for a single ride, with day passes available for $13.

Buses & Shuttles:

The **Deuce** bus is a cheap way to travel up and down the Strip, and the **RTC Transit System** also services areas beyond the Strip, including Fremont Street and the airport.

Rideshare & Taxis

Uber & Lyft:

Rideshare services are easy to use in Las Vegas, with dedicated pickup zones at most hotels and the airport. They're usually cheaper than taxis for short trips.

Taxis:

Taxis are readily available but can be more expensive. There's also a $3 surcharge for airport pickups.

Tips for First-Timers

Avoid Long Walks in the Heat:

Even if attractions look close on a map, distances can be deceiving. Use the monorail or rideshare services to save time and energy, especially in the hot summer months.

Overpaying for Transportation:

Always check prices on rideshare apps before booking, especially during peak times when surge pricing can increase fares.

Staying Safe: Common Scams & How to Avoid Them

While Las Vegas is generally a safe destination, there are a few common scams that first-time visitors should be aware of. Here's a guide to the most frequent scams and how to avoid them.

Timeshare Scams

How It Works:

Timeshare salespeople often approach tourists with offers for free show tickets, dinners, or other perks in exchange for attending a "short" presentation. These presentations can last hours, and the sales pressure is intense.

How to Avoid:

Politely decline any offers of "free" perks that require attending a presentation, and don't provide personal information to anyone offering such deals.

Street Performers & Characters

How It Works:

You'll find street performers and costumed characters along the Strip offering to take photos with you. Afterward, they may demand a tip, often more than expected.

How to Avoid:

If you're not interested in paying, avoid taking photos with performers. If you do take a picture, be prepared to tip (around $5 is standard).

Overpriced 'VIP' Services

How It Works:

Scammers may offer you "VIP" access to clubs or events at inflated prices. These "services" are often not legitimate, and you may end up paying more than necessary for entry.

How to Avoid:

Book VIP services directly through the club or hotel. Avoid offers from street vendors or unsolicited offers from strangers.

What to Do if You Feel Pressured:

- If someone is pressuring you into a sale or offer, walk away. Don't feel obligated to engage, and trust your instincts if something feels off.

By staying aware of these common scams, you'll be able to enjoy your Las Vegas trip safely and with peace of mind.

CHAPTER 13: HIDDEN GEMS: LAS VEGAS OFF THE BEATEN PATH

Discovering Local Hangouts

While most visitors flock to the Las Vegas Strip, locals know the best spots to relax, eat, and unwind away from the tourist-heavy areas. Here's a guide to some of the favorite local hangouts where you can experience the 'real' Las Vegas.

Downtown Las Vegas

Evel Pie:

Located on Fremont Street, **Evel Pie** is a quirky pizzeria dedicated to daredevil Evel Knievel. Locals love this spot for its laid-back vibe, arcade games, and delicious slices served by the slice or pie. It's a go-to for those looking to grab a drink and enjoy a fun, low-key evening.

PublicUs:

A favorite coffee shop for locals, **PublicUs** offers a cozy atmosphere with artisanal coffee, fresh pastries, and a rotating menu of globally inspired dishes. The inviting, minimalist space is perfect for relaxing or catching up on work while enjoying great food and friendly service.

The Arts District

ReBAR:

ReBAR in the Arts District is a local hangout combining a neighborhood bar with a vintage shop. You can enjoy a drink while browsing unique items for sale. The atmosphere is casual and welcoming, and the bar often hosts art exhibits, live music, and local events.

Esther's Kitchen:

Known for its Italian comfort food and house-made pasta, **Esther's Kitchen** is a beloved eatery where locals gather for delicious, farm-to-table meals. Located in the Arts District, this restaurant is perfect for a laid-back dining experience with exceptional food.

Neighborhood Bars & Hidden Gems

The Sand Dollar Lounge:

Tucked away from the Strip, **The Sand Dollar Lounge** is a vintage dive bar with live blues music, a laid-back crowd, and strong drinks. It's a great spot for those who want to escape the tourist scene and enjoy a more authentic Vegas nightlife experience.

Velveteen Rabbit:

This bohemian cocktail bar in the Arts District is a local favorite for its creative drinks and eclectic decor. **Velveteen Rabbit** offers a rotating seasonal cocktail menu, and the relaxed vibe makes it a perfect spot for those seeking something unique and intimate.

Unique Attractions

If you're looking for something a little offbeat and memorable, Las Vegas has plenty of unique attractions that go beyond the usual casino and nightlife experiences.

Neon Boneyard (Neon Museum)

Overview:

The **Neon Museum**, also known as the Neon Boneyard, is home to an incredible collection of historic neon signs from old Las Vegas casinos and businesses. These massive, colorful signs offer a glimpse into the city's rich past, making it a must-see for history buffs and anyone fascinated by Vegas's iconic glitz.

Why It's Special:

The museum preserves Las Vegas's neon legacy, with guided tours that provide fascinating stories behind the signs. At night, the **Brilliant!** light show brings some of the signs back to life through projection mapping, creating a magical experience you won't find anywhere else.

Tips for Visiting:

Book tickets in advance, as the museum's tours often sell out. Sunset and evening tours offer the most striking views, with the signs illuminated against the night sky.

Pinball Hall of Fame

Overview:

A paradise for retro gaming fans, the **Pinball Hall of Fame** houses hundreds of pinball machines dating back to the 1950s. This interactive museum lets visitors play vintage games, making it both a nostalgic trip and a fun experience for people of all ages.

Why It's Special:

With an impressive collection of machines spanning decades, from classic pinball to old arcade games, the Hall of Fame offers something unique for visitors looking to take a break from the traditional Vegas attractions.

Tips for Visiting:

Admission is free, and you only pay for the games you play. Be sure to bring quarters (or exchange cash on-site), and take your time exploring the rare and unusual machines.

The Best Vintage Shopping & Thrift Finds

Las Vegas offers a treasure trove of vintage and thrift shopping experiences, perfect for those looking to score one-of-a-kind pieces and retro gems.

Downtown Arts District

Antique Alley Mall:

Located in the heart of the Arts District, **Antique Alley Mall** is a sprawling marketplace featuring dozens of vendors selling vintage clothing, furniture, jewelry, and more. It's the perfect spot for anyone on the hunt for unique finds and hidden treasures.

Patina Décor:

This boutique specializes in mid-century modern furniture and decor, attracting vintage lovers and design enthusiasts alike. **Patina Décor** offers a curated selection of vintage furniture, lighting, and home accessories that bring a touch of retro Vegas into your home.

Fremont Street & Beyond

Buffalo Exchange:

Known for its eclectic mix of second-hand clothing, **Buffalo Exchange** on Fremont Street is a favorite for those seeking affordable, fashionable pieces. The shop stocks everything from retro T-shirts to designer labels, making it a must-stop for thrifters.

Gypsy Den Vintage:

A quirky shop offering everything from bohemian fashion to retro furniture, **Gypsy Den** is a great place for browsing and discovering unique, hand-picked vintage pieces. The shop's fun, eclectic vibe makes it a great spot for finding clothing and accessories with character.

Alternative Las Vegas

Las Vegas is home to an array of quirky museums and offbeat attractions that cater to those seeking something different from the typical tourist experience.

Burlesque Hall of Fame

Overview:

Celebrating the art of burlesque, the **Burlesque Hall of Fame** features costumes, props, and memorabilia from the world's greatest burlesque performers. The museum traces the history of this seductive art form and its influence on Vegas's entertainment scene.

Why It's Special:

The exhibits provide a deeper look at the glamorous, often misunderstood world of burlesque. Visitors can learn about the performers who shaped this art form and see rare artifacts from its golden age.

Who It Appeals To:

Perfect for lovers of theater, history, and Vegas's vibrant entertainment history, the Burlesque Hall of Fame offers an alternative view of the city's past.

Erotic Heritage Museum

Overview:

The **Erotic Heritage Museum** is a one-of-a-kind space dedicated to the history and cultural impact of human sexuality. Featuring exhibits that span art, literature, and science, the museum covers everything from ancient erotic art to modern-day cultural shifts in attitudes toward sex.

Why It's Special:

With a mission to educate and inform in an open, inclusive manner, the museum explores an important aspect of human history often overlooked in traditional museums.

Who It Appeals To:

This museum is perfect for adults interested in a more intellectual, nontraditional take on sexuality and its role in human culture. It's a thought-provoking and often surprising experience.

Meow Wolf's Omega Mart

Overview: Meow Wolf's Omega Mart is an immersive art installation that takes visitors on a surreal journey through a seemingly ordinary grocery store that hides secret doors, otherworldly realms, and interactive art.

Why It's Special:

Omega Mart defies explanation, offering visitors a chance to interact with art in a playful, mind-bending environment. Each room reveals something new, and the experience is filled with Easter eggs and puzzles to discover.

Who It Appeals To:

Ideal for those seeking an immersive, interactive art experience, Omega Mart is great for families, artists, and anyone looking to explore their curiosity in a fun and unusual setting.

These alternative attractions show a completely different side of Las Vegas, one that goes beyond the surface to offer unique, unforgettable experiences for visitors eager to explore the city's quirky, creative, and unconventional side.

CHAPTER 14: TRAVELER RESOURCES & USEFUL CONTACTS

Emergency Information & Important Numbers

Traveling to Las Vegas is usually a fun and exciting experience, but it's always good to be prepared in case of an emergency. Here is a detailed list of essential emergency contacts and important numbers for quick access to help during your stay.

Emergency Services

- **911**: For emergencies requiring police, fire, or medical assistance.
- **Las Vegas Metropolitan Police Department (Non-Emergency Line)**: +1 (702) 828-3111
    - For non-emergencies, such as reporting minor accidents or suspicious activity.
- **Fire Department (Non-Emergency Line)**: +1 (702) 383-2888
    - For non-emergency fire department services or general inquiries.

24/7 Taxi Services

- **Yellow Checker Star Cab**: +1 (702) 873-2000
- **Desert Cab**: +1 (702) 386-9102
    - Available 24/7, these taxi services can be called if rideshare apps are unavailable.

Tow Truck Services

- **United Roadside Assistance**: +1 (702) 433-5823
- **Elite Towing**: +1 (702) 383-3278
    - In case of car trouble or accidents, these services provide towing and roadside assistance.

Lost & Found Departments

- **Las Vegas Strip Hotels & Casinos**:
    - Each major hotel and casino has its lost-and-found department. Contact the front desk or concierge to inquire about lost items.
- **McCarran International Airport (Lost & Found)**: +1 (702) 261-5134
    - For any lost belongings within the airport.

Having these contacts on hand ensures that you're well-prepared in case of any emergency or unexpected situation during your trip.

Local Medical Facilities & Pharmacies

If you experience an illness or injury during your trip, there are numerous medical facilities and pharmacies across Las Vegas that cater to tourists. Here's a guide to the best places to seek medical attention or fill prescriptions.

Urgent Care Centers

Southwest Medical Urgent Care (West Charleston):

- +1 (702) 877-8600
- 4835 S. Fort Apache Rd, Las Vegas, NV 89147
- **Hours**: 8 AM - 8 PM, 7 days a week
- Located near the Strip, this urgent care center is ideal for non-life-threatening conditions like minor injuries, flu symptoms, and allergies.

U.S. HealthWorks Urgent Care (South Las Vegas):

- +1 (702) 734-4452
- 3830 E. Flamingo Rd, Las Vegas, NV 89121
- **Hours**: 7 AM - 7 PM, Monday - Friday
- A popular choice for travelers needing immediate care.

Hospitals

University Medical Center (UMC):

- +1 (702) 383-2000
- 1800 W. Charleston Blvd, Las Vegas, NV 89102
- A full-service hospital with a 24-hour emergency room, UMC is located close to the Strip and is known for its exceptional trauma care.

Sunrise Hospital & Medical Center:

- +1 (702) 731-8000
- 3186 S. Maryland Pkwy, Las Vegas, NV 89109
- One of the largest hospitals in Las Vegas, offering a wide range of medical services, including a 24-hour emergency department.

24-Hour Pharmacies

Walgreens (Las Vegas Blvd & Flamingo):

- +1 (702) 732-2507
- 3765 S. Las Vegas Blvd, Las Vegas, NV 89109
- **Open 24/7**
- Conveniently located on the Strip for any last-minute prescriptions or over-the-counter medication needs.

CVS Pharmacy (Near the Strip):

- +1 (702) 866-2350
- 3758 S. Las Vegas Blvd, Las Vegas, NV 89109
- **Open 24/7**
- This pharmacy offers a range of medications, snacks, and travel essentials, with a convenient location near major hotels.

For added convenience, both **Walgreens** and **CVS** offer prescription delivery services to your hotel if needed.

Helpful Apps for Navigating Las Vegas

To make your trip to Las Vegas smoother and more enjoyable, consider downloading these helpful apps. From navigating transportation to booking restaurants and shows, these apps provide essential tools to help you get the most out of your stay.

Transportation Apps

Uber / Lyft:

- Available for iOS & Android
- These popular rideshare apps allow you to easily book a ride anywhere in Las Vegas, including from McCarran Airport or along the Strip.

Las Vegas Monorail App:

- Available for iOS & Android
- This app offers real-time updates, maps, and ticket purchasing for the Las Vegas Monorail, which runs between major hotels on the Strip.

Dining & Entertainment Apps

OpenTable:

- Available for iOS & Android
- Use this app to book reservations at the best restaurants in Las Vegas. It's especially useful for securing a spot at popular dining destinations on the Strip.

Yelp:

- Available for iOS & Android
- Perfect for finding reviews and recommendations on local dining, attractions, and services in Las Vegas. Use it to discover hidden gems and local favorites.

Events & Show Apps

Vegas.com:

- Available for iOS & Android

- This app provides real-time updates on shows, concerts, and events happening in Las Vegas. It's great for purchasing last-minute tickets or exploring new entertainment options.

TodayTix:

- Available for iOS & Android
- Another useful app for finding deals on Las Vegas shows performances, and attractions, often offering same-day tickets at a discount.

Hotel Booking Apps

Hotels.com:

- Available for iOS & Android
- Book hotel rooms with ease and find last-minute deals on accommodations in Las Vegas.

Airbnb:

- Available for iOS & Android
- If you're looking for unique, non-hotel accommodations, Airbnb is a great way to find vacation rentals in and around Las Vegas.

These apps are essential for making the most of your time in Las Vegas, whether you're planning your next meal, booking a show, or navigating the city efficiently.

Consular Services & Travel Assistance

International travelers visiting Las Vegas should know where to find consular services in case of emergencies, such as lost passports, legal issues, or health concerns. Here's a guide to the consular services and travel assistance available in Las Vegas.

Consular Services

United States Embassy & Consulates Directory:

- For international visitors, the **U.S. Department of State** provides an online directory to locate your country's nearest consulate in Las Vegas or surrounding areas.
- Visit the official website: https://www.usembassy.gov

Consulate of Mexico in Las Vegas:

- +1 (702) 477-2727
- 823 S. 6th St, Las Vegas, NV 89101
- Offers assistance to Mexican nationals in cases involving lost passports, emergency documents, and legal advice.

Consulate of Canada in Los Angeles (Nearest to Las Vegas):

- +1 (844) 880-6519
- 550 S. Hope St, Los Angeles, CA 90071
- The Canadian Consulate assists with passports, emergency travel documents, and consular protection.

Canadian citizens can also access services by contacting their consulate by phone.

Travel Assistance Services

Lost Luggage Assistance:

- If your luggage goes missing, contact the **McCarran International Airport Lost & Found**:
- +1 (702) 261-5134

Travel Insurance Claims:

- If you've purchased travel insurance, most providers have 24-hour assistance services. Be sure to have your policy number and contact details handy in case of emergencies.

Legal Advice & Travel Documentation:

- Most consulates can provide information on legal aid in case of arrest, accident, or other legal issues. They can also assist with temporary travel documents in case of lost or stolen passports.

These consular services and travel assistance resources are here to help international visitors feel safe, supported, and informed during their stay in Las Vegas.

CONCLUSION

Thank you for choosing *The Las Vegas Pocket Guide 2025* as your companion for touring one of the world's most exciting cities. I'm thrilled that you trusted this guide to help shape your adventure, whether it's your first time visiting Las Vegas or a return trip to rediscover its vibrant energy. This guide was written with your experience in mind, designed to not only lead you through the glittering lights of the Strip but also to help you uncover the hidden gems that make Las Vegas truly unforgettable.

Throughout this book, we've covered the essentials of planning and maximizing your trip. From must-see attractions like the Bellagio Fountains, Fremont Street Experience, and the high-energy shows that define Las Vegas entertainment, to the lesser-known gems like the Neon Museum and the peaceful escape of Red Rock Canyon, this guide has aimed to give you a well-rounded view of what the city has to offer.

We explored the best places to stay, from luxurious hotels on the Strip to budget-friendly options that don't compromise on quality. You've learned where to find world-class dining, whether you're seeking fine dining experiences at Michelin-starred restaurants or classic comfort foods from hidden local spots. The book also introduced you to the city's rich history and culture through its museums, art installations, and even day trips to the Grand Canyon and Hoover Dam, showcasing the natural beauty just beyond the city.

For nightlife lovers, we dove into the best spots for drinks, music, and dancing, while also guiding you through quieter, more intimate experiences for those seeking a relaxed evening. Whether it's shopping at the Forum Shops or unwinding at a spa, I hope you've found plenty of options to make your Vegas trip exactly what you want it to be.

This book has offered insider tips to help you navigate the city like a pro, from getting around efficiently to finding the best times to visit certain attractions. It's also been packed with advice on staying safe and making the most of your time, ensuring that your trip is both enjoyable and stress-free.

As you set out to explore all that Las Vegas has to offer, I want to wish you nothing but the best. May your trip be filled with excitement, discovery, and joy. I pray that you have safe travels, that every moment is filled with new experiences, and that you leave Las Vegas with unforgettable memories. Whether you're here to relax, have fun, or embark on new adventures, I hope this guide has been a helpful companion along the way.

Thank you again for allowing this guide to be part of your journey. Safe travels, and may your time in Las Vegas be everything you've dreamed of and more.